About the Author

Susan Jane Broda Tamburi is a teacher, writer and mother of four. She works in Switzerland and collaborates with the University of Geneva as a teacher trainer. After writing articles for an animal journal as well as a collection of children's stories, she published *Power, Beauty and Legitimacy of Adolescence* in 2019, a book about understanding teenagers.

Encouraged by the success of her first book, she wrote *Teacher's Digest* the following year, expressing the very quintessence of teaching to help people discover if they are made for the profession.

Teacher's Digest

Susan Jane Broda Tamburi

Teacher's Digest

Olympia Publishers
London

www.olympiapublishers.com
OLYMPIA PAPERBACK EDITION

A CIP catalogue record for this title is
available from the British Library.

ISBN: 978-1-80074-212-3

First Published in 2022

Olympia Publishers
Tallis House
2 Tallis Street
London
EC4Y 0AB

Printed in Great Britain

Dedication

I dedicate this book once again to my family, with a special thought for my dearest brother.

The mediocre teacher tells, the good teacher explains, the superior teacher demonstrates, but the best teacher inspires.

Contents

INTRODUCTION

This book is addressed to all teachers, young and old, newcomers to the profession or already experienced ones. It will help people who want to embrace a teaching career decide if this profession is really meant for them. It will also help those who have been teaching for a while and who are eager to keep up to date with the fast-developing educational trends and innovations.

Basing the information on real life experience, the book also offers a survey of the already existing changes in education around the world and shows how teachers have to tailor their practices to ITC (Information Technologies and Communication) and AI (Artificial Intelligence) which are changing their profession in a big way. They will then be able to bridge the gap between traditional and digital teaching harmoniously.

CHAPTER 1
IS TEACHING THE RIGHT PROFESSION
FOR YOU?

At the end of secondary school, the world lies ahead, ready to grasp. Finding the right studies to follow or find a career path to embrace is not an easy task. Some are lucky enough to know exactly what they want to do — or sometimes think they do — but the great majority of students have to go through thorough self-analysis to know what direction to take and which professional field to choose. A fair percentage of students do not know what they want to do later on and many graduates don't follow up with the profession which is directly linked to their training. Knowing what profession to choose is far from easy because many factors play a role, some of which, paradoxically, seldom come into mind.

In my previous book, Power, Beauty and Legitimacy of Adolescence, I speak at length about the importance of taking time finding one's professional orientation basing my conclusions both on the observation of my students and on the findings of famous developmental psychologists. Among them, Erik Erikson and James E. Marcia are those who, in my opinion have shed the most informative light on the subject because they both analyzed in depth the process one goes through when trying to find one's own identity and consequently the best way of deciding on a career. It is a process that needs both a certain amount of time and properly directed reflection.

James E. Marcia studied Vocation Identity Exploration and Self Knowledge. He assessed the process of vocation identity of teenagers on the threshold of adulthood basing his analysis on concepts already identified by Erikson: Crisis, Exploration and Commitment. Marcia devised the Identity Status Interview, a method of semi-structured questionnaires for psychological identity research, that investigates an individual's extent of exploration and commitment in various areas of his or her life. Evaluating the material provided in this interview by using a scoring manual he described four possible identity statuses: foreclosed, diffusion, moratorium, and achieved.

	Low commitment	High commitment
Low crisis exploration	IDENTITY DIFFUSION	IDENTITY FORECLOSURE
High crisis exploration	IDENTITY MORATORIUM	IDENTITY ACHIEVEMENT

Let's apply these conclusions to the specific choice of a teaching career. Identity foreclosure happens when a person prematurely commits to values or roles that others prescribe. The teenager already knows what he wants to do later on, influenced by his or her social environment, parents' opinion and close surroundings. The person has not engaged in any kind of research but follows a family scheme, either willingly or under pressure, without having made any personal choice and without having assessed the correspondences with his own identity or his owns desires. For example, the child of parents who are both teachers may think it normal to become one too. Many of my colleagues' children are also teachers. In some cases, the profession corresponds to the individual, in other cases it is clear that the career choice was greatly influenced by the parents' will.

Marcia also mentions the case of negative-identity which occurs when adolescents purposely adopt an identity which blatantly goes against the one expected by their peer group, thus refusing to become an alter ego of their parents. For example, parents who work in the educational field and who assume implicitly that their children will also follow that path may trigger the opposite response. The youth will then want to engage in a profession that has nothing to do with education, although in some cases it may have ultimately been a good choice.

Identity diffusion occurs when a person lacks a clear sense of self but still hasn't explored issues related to identity development. Some adolescents seem to be overwhelmed by that task and are in a state of procrastination, social isolation and general withdrawal. Such youths may not have experienced an identity crisis, while others show little interest in such matters. A common feature would be recurring indecision. Applied to my topic, it means that the youth would not even make the effort of getting to know anything about the profession of teacher, or of any other profession at that stage.

Identity Moratorium is when a person is delaying commitment to an identity because he or she is experiencing high crisis exploration of various values and roles. More explicitly, identity moratorium is the status of individuals who are actively exploring alternatives. This status which used to be criticised in the past, is nowadays considered a constructive stage in life which can take the form of multiple internships or sabbaticals. Here a student would experience teaching in summer camps or give private lessons, in other words would be experimenting with teaching and the educational field.

Identity achievement occurs when a person considers alternative possibilities and commits to a certain identity and path in life, once a crisis has been experienced and worked through. Marcia considered a likely progression would be from identity diffusion through moratorium to identity achievement. Identity achievement shows that the person has gone through a process of active exploration and has found his own personal identity. It is a positive realisation which is the guarantee of harmony and balance. In the case of teaching, enough experience will have demonstrated that the job is appealing enough to engage into it seriously.

There is one more stage to consider which is called Identity shifts. This last stage of identity achievement does not exclude a change in orientation later on. Transitions are often inspired by a disequilibrium in identity. This crisis in identity can come in the form of various life events. Depending on the individual, particular issues such as death of a loved one, job loss, or moving may cause imbalance. It can lead to what Marcia calls MAMA Circle: Moratorium — Achievement — Moratorium — Achievement. As far as professional choices are concerned, this circle means that a person who has found a profession which corresponds to his or her inner identity could very well want to change direction after a few years of professional engagement by redirecting his or her activity. This can be done for training purposes, improvement, promotion, added interests or social progression.

Let us take the example of a young woman who has chosen the job of primary teacher, which corresponds to her will and desire of helping others. After a few years, she could very well feel unfulfilled by her choice and want to redirect her commitment by following a career in psychology. There is a common ground in her career choice but time and experience are directing her towards what really works best for her.

Whatever the reason for disequilibrium, a period of re-construction begins. During reconstruction a person may regress to an earlier identity status. It is crucial that old constructs fall so that new ones that are more encompassing of the person's identity may be built. In the reconstruction process there is still continuity with the previous identity, however the newer construction is broadened to include new life experiences and commitments.

In conclusion, if we follow Marcia's theory, it means that we must not decide to embrace the profession of teacher solely because we happen to come from a family of teachers or because our parents want us to work in education. It also means that a person who is thinking of becoming one should be ready to give himself or herself the chance of experimenting with the profession to see what happens in reality and to evaluate both the requirements linked to the job and personal qualities and skills, to see if they match.

So when does one really know when a career choice is the right one? Some people go through life without really knowing or not even caring. They spend many years just doing what they are used to without thinking of the adequacy of their profession. However, sooner or later the compatibility between the job and the person who is doing it is bound to surface one way or another, and when things are not aligned, it can cause problems from irritability to a more serious existential crisis which can lead to depression or burnout.

Ken Robinson has analyzed this issue in depth in his book The Element. He shows how you know when the job you do corresponds to your inner being. In other words when your professional activity is the one that was just cut out for you. The answer is very simple: it is when a very subtle combination takes place between something you are good at and something you are actually passionate about. When both skills and passion are reunited, you know that your choice is a good one. Let us analyse this more in detail.

Basing his findings on real life experience, Ken Robinson shows that there are people who are good at some things but don't necessarily like doing them, and others who would love to engage in a certain kind of professional activity but are not good at it. He says that you reach a level of bliss only when both coincide: the skills and the passion. This is what he calls "the Element". But there is another aspect to be considered, and that is time. This is important for two reasons, firstly you need time to see if the professional activity you are engaged in satisfies you and secondly you need to practice it long enough to be good at it.

So if personal blossoming comes when innate skills meet passion it means that one has to find a job which combines natural abilities and something one loves doing. This is not always easy. Many people choose a job in which they excel but with time they realise that if asked, they don't really like what they do and similarly, some people do what they like to do but eventually realise that others are performing far better than they are.

You will not know straight away if you were meant to be a teacher because, as Ken Robinson puts it, personal skills and passion are organic. They grow and develop with time. You have to experience teaching for a while to see if the activity coincides with your inner-self. You must also work hard to learn how to improve your teaching skills, how to handle children or teenagers and so on. It is a long process.

What Ken Robinson says about self-realization has to be understood in two ways when adapted to my topic. Firstly, if you want to become a teacher and a good one, some things have to be innate. You will learn many tricks of the trade and lots of didactic and methodological theories along the way but at the same time there has to be something in you that will make you good at your job and passionate about it.

In my experience, all the people who think teaching is easy change their minds one month into the profession. As the saying goes. "Teaching is hard because it matters". Similarly, all the good teachers I know have something in common, like a trade mark. They are recognisable in a million. They all have the basic pre-requisites I will be talking about in the next chapter.

Marcia's theory shows that one can very well experience being a teacher for a few months or years and then have second thoughts about it. This is not a problem, on the contrary. If you realise you don't want to follow through, you have to ask yourself why you were attracted to the profession in the first place because this is going to give you an important clue into discovering the truth about yourself. The choice you made originally indicates something about you that you need to analyse and understand.

You can be skilled at teaching a subject without liking what you do and you can be passionate about wanting to teach and not be good at it. Most frustrated teachers, and I have met a lot of them, continue doing their job because they feel it is too late in life to change their career course but they hate every day of their work. Students are very good at recognising that kind of teacher and, more often than not, will give them a hard time which makes the situation even worse. The students feel they have been cheated on, having been attributed a teacher who doesn't really care and the teacher feels worse every year because he or she feels that the connection with the students is not working.

It is never too late to change. If you like working with teenagers but you don't like teaching them a subject, you may then go onto another profession involving social exchange, which you may like more. You will be redirecting your choice by establishing another kind of relationship with them, like medical or psychological care or coaching them in other domains like sports or arts. There are many jobs related to working with children and young adults that do not require being in front of a large group of them in one location, trying to pass on to them an educational message. This is what I mentioned earlier, and that Marcia calls, identity shift. A re-refocusing of one's choices based on a better understanding of one's identity. This is also the best guarantee of a successful career. I once met a teacher who changed the course of her career becoming a social assistant, a choice she never regretted.

Looking back, if I adapt both Marcia's and Robinson's theories to my personal experience, everything falls into place as I shall demonstrate in the next chapter.

CHAPTER 2
PERSONAL EXPERIENCE
How I came to teaching

I was brought up in a family that did not impose any career frame neither on me nor on my brother. My parents were wise enough to let us discover what we wanted to do and supported us even if we made changes in the course of our studies. Their sole objective was our wellbeing and they did everything to help us achieve it. I will always remember my brother coming home one day, after two years of studying biology saying, "Mum, Dad I have decided to stop my science studies and am going to study economics and statistics to become an actuary." My parents instantly gave him the moral support he needed and he never regretted his decision.

As far as I was concerned, I remember being puzzled when thinking about what I wanted to do after my baccalaureate diploma. I knew that I was interested in all that had to do with children or the animal world. I also knew that I wanted to help both in one way or another. Pediatrician or veterinarian seemed to be good options. As I was not really good at maths, physics or chemistry, my parents suggested that I did an internship in a veterinarian practice during the summer vacations to see if I liked it. They knew me more than I did at that stage and made that suggestion to help me discover more about myself.

I managed to find an internship for one month at a vet's practice in Eastbourne, Sussex, where we usually went on holiday to visit my grandparents. My job during the first week was going to be to help out cleaning the cages and the waiting room. However, on the very first day, quite unexpectedly, the vet asked me if I wanted to stay in the room while he was going to perform an operation. I eagerly accepted, excited that my training seemed to be going faster than expected. The scheduled operation, was the spaying of a female cocker spaniel. The dog was anaesthetised, then was laid on its back. The hair was shaved on its belly. When the vet slit open the lower part of the stomach with a scalpel, I fainted instantly.

When I came to, staff were giving me sugared tea and waving bath salts under my nose. Everyone thought I had blacked out because it was my first time, so next day, I was asked again if I wanted to be in the operating room for the next intervention. Again, I accepted, wanting so much to be up to it. This time it was a boxer that had to be castrated because he was too aggressive. The exact same thing happened, I collapsed as soon as the scalpel touched its skin. From that moment onwards I was asked to do minor chores like walking dogs and feeding the animals.

The second week I remember opening a trash bin and seeing two dead cats lying there, stiff, among the garbage. I was told that the owner decided to euthanize them because they were getting too old and he didn't want to look after them any more. I was shocked both by this decision and the fact of seeing the cats just thrown in a bin.

I didn't manage to hold out the whole month. I realised that the profession of veterinarian was not only extremely demanding on an academic level in subjects I was not even good at, but more importantly, the emotional aspect of the activity did not coincide with my sensitivity.

I have felt empathic or, more precisely, over-empathic from a very early age and thought that this quality was the main asset needed to be a good vet. Obviously, I was wrong. I would never have been able to euthanize any animal, I would just have adopted them all, one after the other... Vets and doctors have to be emotionally strong at all times and I knew that I was not that kind of person, consequently I ruled out medical school too.

My second attempt at trying to find a professional orientation was when I joined the Art and Design school in Eastbourne. My mother was an artist and as I was good at drawing and painting, I gave it a shot. I quite enjoyed what I was doing but after a few months I didn't really see the outcome of just painting beautiful still life or naked models. When having to choose a department to specialize in during the second semester, I chose graphic design only because there was an incredibly handsome student working there. It was clear that although the teachers said I had good potential, I had chosen art for all the wrong reasons and the studies were not satisfying me because they were not quenching my thirst neither for social interaction nor for altruism. I then decided that art would be something I would do on the side but would not be my real job later on.

It so happened that just as I was having doubts about my motivation, I received a phone call from Switzerland. A family crisis called me back to Geneva and I decided to quit my art studies that same day to the amazement of my teachers. So I settled back in my home country to deal with what was going on there. As for my studies, I only had two weeks left to register at Geneva University before the closing date. I remember going to the admissions office with my French boyfriend. He had given up his first year of medical studies in Grenoble. Although our respective first attempts at studies had failed for very different reasons, at least we were together again, enjoying a fusional relationship. We were two naïve teenagers knowing we wanted to study, neither of us having a clue about which subject to choose.

At that time applications were not made via an online platform. I can still picture us standing awkwardly in front of the admissions officer who was becoming impatient. I suddenly made a rash decision, saying, "Okay, I speak French, English and Italian and the only option that fits is *Lettres* in which we have to choose three subjects so English, French and Italian literature are going to be my options." I had absolutely no idea about what profession could be linked to those choices but I had to put my name down for something.

My friend was still confused in front of the list of options so I literally decided for him: "You like numbers, don't you?" I asked him. "Okay, so take *Sciences Economiques*, with the option *Méthodes Quantitatives*."

"Whatever for?" he asked.

"Because I heard that you have a better salary if that is added to your diploma title." I answered.

"Okay," he nodded, incredulously.

And so we enrolled, two blindfolded youths going on a mystery journey. Luckily, he enjoyed the course but regularly told me with a deep frown that the option I had chosen for him made all the exams much more difficult. Ultimately, he passed them. He was grateful and thanked me in the end. It so happened that he later became a highly qualified financial analyst. I had hit the nail on the head by pure chance.

As for me, I literally discovered that I adored studying literature, not knowing or even caring at that stage what professional door this would open. Looking back, it did make sense as my best marks at school had always been linked to languages or literature, but at the time I had never given it a second thought.

I started giving private English and French lessons to individual students at home to make a little pocket money. Then came an opportunity: a friend asked me if I wanted to replace him for his evening class. He taught English to adults. I accepted mainly because I felt uncomfortable refusing. I was awfully nervous that first evening. To my surprise, the course went fine and I found the students very endearing. As things had gone smoothly, and that, apparently, the students had appreciated the course, my friend jumped on the opportunity to ask me if I wanted to take on the group entirely as his girlfriend was going to Germany and he wanted to follow her. So I applied for the job officially and got regular evening classes which financed part of my studies. Once I got my master's degree, I went on to teacher training and worked in a secondary school. I am still working in the same school now so many years later. The school has become much larger since, including all kinds of students from regular ones to apprentices. They range from fifteen to twenty years old and we sometimes have older ones too. I kept on teaching adults for many years and I am now part of the school management. I am responsible for the training of new teachers, and enjoying every minute of it.

So it is by pure chance that I started teaching. Why did this profession suit me? Why did I want to continue in that field? How did it correspond to my personality, my inner-self and my conscious or still unconscious goals in life? Although I seemed to go about it the wrong way around, the profession happened to coincide with something deep inside of me that I got to understood only much later. I wanted to do a job that entailed helping others, working and interacting with human beings. A job in which I would feel needed and useful. Teaching fulfilled that.

So if we apply what James E. Marcia and Ken Robinson say about the choice of a career to my experience one can say that both theories have proved right. Let's analyse this step by step.

Firstly, I was not in a situation of identity foreclosure in which my parents pushed me towards a job, I was not influenced by my entourage either. I was given the total freedom of choosing my studies and my career.

Secondly, I put myself in the state of identity moratorium, when I started experimenting in a vet's practice to understand more about myself, my weaknesses and my vulnerability. By accepting the proposition of my German friend, I gave myself yet another opportunity to experiment. The difference this time is that it was my strengths that were being put into light not my weaknesses. So although it was accidentally that I was introduced to teaching, it started to reveal important parts of my personality because, for some reason, I was getting a lot of pleasure out of it.

Finally, the fact of being in an intellectual environment and in contact with tremendously interesting academics at university revealed and developed my love for literature that had been lying dormant. I had always enjoyed analyzing situations and people and now I was applying this to characters in books. I was enjoying this very much. It suddenly all came together and made sense. All the lights were green and I knew I was on the right track.

So when one adds all this up, the conclusion is that I had what it took to become a teacher and accepted putting a lot of work into reaching a level in which I felt comfortable and at ease in my activity, because as Ken Robinson says, passion is not enough, you need hard work. This is an ingredient that was added when I followed a tough two-year teacher training course and put a lot of effort in understanding the methodology and didactic theories. I was amazed at how many things I was learning every day. At that time, I experimented with a variety of pupils including young children, apprentice policemen, commercial employees, teenagers, university students as well as adults, all ranging from beginner to proficiency levels.

But while teaching can certainly be a rewarding career, it is also one of the most challenging ones out there. Although I found the course and the practical experience very interesting, I also found that being assessed constantly in front of a class was extremely stressful. Being observed so narrowly makes you learn a lot about yourself, mainly what you do wrong. And this constant exposure to the eyes of others is something many people cannot deal with. Fortunately, I was open enough to criticism to get through my two years training. I try not to forget how I used to feel when I assess new teachers today.

Another experience gave me the final indication that teaching was the thing for me. During the summer months, I used to work as a secretary for my father, typing letters and dealing with the administration in his office. I was in a very privileged situation, with the perfect boss and a salary which was twice as much as any regular secretary would get. No stress, no fixed schedule, paid meals, total freedom, what more could I ask for? Yet, strangely, I felt frustrated. It is at that point that I discovered another aspect of my personality which also fitted in with the teaching profession. I was spending long days in front of my computer dealing with correspondence and mail and I missed human contact terribly. I didn't even have any calls to make, it was just me and the computer for hours on end. I then realised that a good job for me definitely had to include daily social contact. I needed to talk to people, listen to them, exchange thoughts and opinions. The other thing I was missing was control. I was doing what I was told, I had no initiative in the job, just executing things one after the other, no creativity either (the one thing that was fulfilled in Art School). Teaching includes all of that when planning lessons, choosing books to read and to put it simply, being in charge.

My American partner was the first person to put into words one aspect of my personality that I hadn't really acknowledged before, saying that I am a power and control person. So although I am not a control freak, I do admit I like the freedom of doing things my way and this is also very compatible with the teaching profession.

CHAPTER 3
PREREQUISITES FOR BECOMING A TEACHER

Most people who have never taught imagine that it is easy and don't understand why teachers often seem to be tired despite so many holidays and free time. I hear this all the time. So what makes this job so badly understood by the community? It might be because people think that teaching is just transmitting knowledge, which it is not. Teaching is a creative profession, it is facilitating and provoking a learning process in your students. And this is much harder to achieve, although people who are meant to be teachers will do this naturally with time. What goes on between a student and a teacher is something beyond the subject matter taught. It is the will of learning combined with the will of teaching. One without the other has no sense. To illustrate this, I shall give the example of three teachers I had when I was young.

The two things my maths teacher taught me was first, that appearance matters. She had absolutely no taste in clothing or colour combination and always looked an utter mess. This was such a distraction for me that I could not concentrate on the subject matter. Secondly, that you can be called a teacher without being able to teach. I didn't learn anything in maths and I have been miserably bad at it up to now. She never explained anything clearly, we just had to learn things by heart with no clear understanding. She managed to make me hate anything related to numbers up to this very day.

I didn't learn a lot about biology from my biology teacher either but he taught me so much more in other fields and I have always been grateful for this. He taught me curiosity and more importantly respect for living creatures, a notion that I had always had in me but that he somehow validated. Despite the fact that my marks in biology were more than often below average, I enjoyed his lessons very much.

My literature teacher taught me the world, not only about her subject but about life on a grand scale. This is the domain in which I literally thrived. I shall always be thankful to her for her inspiration. She almost always came in class unprepared, sometimes even forgetting which book we were reading, but as soon as she started talking about literature, characters, style and so on, I was mesmerised. She was very funny too and not authoritative at all, she didn't have to be, all the class was under her spell.

So what is it that makes a teacher unforgettable, for the better or for the worse? And what makes good teachers so special?

There are some undeniable aptitudes that a person has to have if he or she wants to become a teacher. Aptitudes represent the raw matter that you are composed of, they are part of your basic potential. In this chapter I will enumerate, one by one, the main aptitudes needed. They are all equally important to me and the lack of even just one of them could be, in my opinion, detrimental to a career in education. If one wants to feel happy and fulfilled as a teacher, one has to fill all these conditions.

First of all, let us clarify the terminology I am going to

use. One must not confuse aptitude with ability. Abilities need an environment to be able to develop. For example, if you have a good aptitude communicating with teenagers and children but you are very rarely in a situation where you meet them or work with them, you can't practice and develop your aptitude into a well-built ability. What I mean by aptitude could also be called soft skills. Abilities usually require a considerable amount of practice, education or apprenticeship to fully develop. The best way to differentiate the two notions is that if you say I am good at understanding biology for example you are talking about an aptitude, if you say I am an experienced surgeon you are defining abilities. Soft skills can be seen as character traits or interpersonal aptitudes that affect your ability to work and interact with others. They relate to emotional intelligence and are often "people" skills. These soft skills are usually useful for all types of professions. Hard skills on the other hand are usually job specific that can be learned through training, based on technical knowledge.

The hard skills are more or less easy to acquire according to one's own aptitudes, character and personality. For example, if you have the basic aptitudes for being a teacher you will develop them little by little into abilities with experience and in the process, you will learn more about your subject matter, how to be organised, and to plan your courses and so on.

Soft skills are associated with communication, teamwork, adaptability and problem solving, creativity, interpersonal skills, time management, leadership and work ethic. Each category has subdivisions. For creativity we will find divergent thinking, imagination and so forth.

In today's job market, the deciding factor for employers often comes down to a battle between the hard versus soft skills of different candidates. A majority of CEOs believe that soft skills are more important to the success of their business than hard skills. Ideally hard skills and soft skills should complement each other.

My objective is not to merely enumerate a long list of soft skills without further explanation. A catalogue of abstract terms will not help you know if teaching is for you. This is why I am going to use more than one-word terminology in my list. How do you know if you are adaptable or creative if the notions are not linked to what is going to be asked of you in a specific profession? Being creative as an architect or as a teacher is based on a similar skill but this ability branches out in different directions according to one's craft.

I would like to add that the very good teachers I have known, when I was a student at school or at university or even later when I became a teacher myself, all have the following aptitudes which they developed with time into strong abilities. These teachers thrive in their job and you notice them a mile away. Most of their students are inspired by them and will remember them for a very long time.

Here are the basic aptitudes.

Loving people.

You can't become involved in teaching if you don't love people. Working with them, observing them, listening to them understanding them and wanting to share experiences with them. Human contact must be a strong motivating factor. You see this in the way teachers speak about their students, their colleagues and everybody they encounter in their profession or in everyday life. They usually praise their colleagues and students and always find the good side to people. Those who always criticize others should change paths right away. Teaching is a job which entails exchange, if you don't like the people you are going to work with, you are likely to find satisfaction in a more solitary profession. Loving people also means being energized by them. I appreciate the palpable exchange of energies I feel when in front of a group of teenagers. It is both positive and vitalizing.

Loving the subject you teach.

Obviously, you cannot teach a subject that you don't know, but more importantly that you don't like. It is your passion that will be the essential drive and which will enable you to transmit your knowledge to others. If you just know your subject well but are neutral about it, you may become a teacher, but a boring one. It means you have only answered the question "What shall I teach?". But you also have to ask yourself "How shall I teach it?" and when you get even more mature you will be asking the question: "Who am I and how can my inner-self contribute to my teaching?" As the saying goes, "No one should teach who is not in love with teaching".

Acknowledging your limits.

Subjects we teach evolve all the time and are as large and as complex as life itself. We can just attempt to grasp part of them. It is a total illusion to think that one day we will master our subject one hundred per cent, whether it is literature, mathematics or any other topic. No matter how long we study, train or do research, teaching requires a command of content that is impossible to attain. Added to that we have to accept the fact that the people we are teaching are also ever changing. As Parker J. Palmer puts it: the fusion between comprehensive knowledge of the subject we are teaching and total mastery of our audience is impossible to achieve. So the quicker we understand this the more serene we will be. The important thing to remember is that we are not teaching only a subject, we are teaching awareness and enjoying the concept of learning itself.

<u>Understanding that teaching is a truly human activity which emerges from our inner-self.</u>

That's why self-knowledge is as important as knowledge of the subject taught, knowledge of teaching techniques and knowledge of the public we are addressing. You teach what you are. I will go even further, in my experience, it was often students who helped me understand who I am deep inside. For example, one day, when watching the film in class based on the novel The Great Gatsby, I couldn't help but shed a few tears. One student noticed this and said, "Why are you crying? You knew this passage was coming, you made us read the book! Don't be so affected, it is just a movie." Yes indeed, it was just a movie and it was just an adaptation of a book I knew inside out, but that particular scene triggered my sensitivity and still does. To my great amazement, none of the teenagers in the class were feeling as emotional. Unlike me, they all managed to separate fiction from reality. The sequence in the film did not resonate with them like it did with me.

Another occasion was when I had chosen a selection of

five short stories to read for the first semester. When I handed out the fifth one, a student put up his hand and said, "Are you a feminist?" I was taken aback because I was not expecting such a question and in fact I had never really thought about if I was a feminist or not. He continued, "You must be, because all the stories you give us to read, show in some way or another women who have been victims of injustice." The student was absolutely right. But I had made my selection without consciously realising what I was doing. I had already ordered the book we were going to read for the following semester: The Awakening by Kate Chopin! So teaching is by no means an innocent act, it reveals a lot about your inner self, your unconscious feelings and sometimes your hidden fears.

Realising that personal growth is inseparable from education.

One without the other has no sense. Our job is not just to feed the brains of our pupils, it is also to contribute to their personal growth and to ours. Teaching and learning are inseparable. By teaching you learn. By learning you need to share. There is no hierarchy between the teacher and the learner. We are all equal travelers on some kind of intellectual voyage. This sensation of fulfillness is very well expressed by Parker:

J. Palmer in The Courage to Teach. He says: I am a teacher at heart, and there are moments in the classroom when I can hardly hold the joy. When my students and I discover unchartered territory to explore, when the pathway out of a thicket opens up before us, when our experience is illumined by the lightening-life of the mind — then teaching is the finest art I know.

<u>Measuring the impact we can have on others.</u>

Teachers' responsibility and influence are enormous. Aside from parents, they are one of the most consistent mentors in a child's life.

That means setting a good example, at all times but also inspiring them, transmitting the best part of what they are. The influence of a good teacher can never be erased. Education shapes an individual allowing creativity, opportunity and growth. So it is not just about being a role model it is about having a big impact on helping shape and support students' strengths and goals in life. If a teacher believes in his student's potential, they will improve their self-perception and academic performance. What a teacher says has immediate consequences because students identify with the beliefs their teachers have on them. They then accept them as part of who they are and start believing in their personal abilities.

I developed this topic in my previous book Power, Beauty and Legitimacy of Adolescence in the chapter on self-concept and self- esteem. In short, unstated or covert messages are powerful. When teachers make students understand that they can achieve a task they will probably perform well, if a teacher implies that the students are no good in such a domain, their performance will be poor.

<u>Including personal involvement in what you do.</u>

Teachers who do the job just for the money or for the amount holidays will become frustrated teachers and this will show sooner or later. They belong to one of the categories of people who usually experience a professional burnout. You can't isolate your life from your teaching profession and vice versa. Some professions are totally separate from everyday life. For example, a bricklayer will not take his work home with him. He might think about the building he is constructing and talk about it at home but his life is separate from the function of bricklaying. Good teachers will notice that there is no clear separation between their everyday personal life and their profession. One grows into the other naturally, they intermingle and coexist. This means that you involve yourself totally in the exchange you have with your students and this interaction doesn't stop once the lesson is over. It affects you consciously or unconsciously.

Embracing diversity and adapting to it.

This goes much further than just adaptability, a soft skill that often comes up during job interviews. Wondering if you are an adaptable kind of person goes much deeper if you are considering a job in education. Indeed, you will have to deal with students of all walks of life, cultures and origins. You will be facing a multiplicity of humors, characters, personalities, dispositions and so on and this on a daily basis.

In sales, employees have to deal with tricky customers and although this can be extremely tiring, ultimately one customer replaces another. Flexibility is taken to another level altogether with teaching. For one whole academic year, educators have to deal with diverse learning abilities and must use multisensory instruction to make sure that they are reaching out to all the students. Some are more visual while others tend to be auditory or tactile. There can also be sequential, global, intuitive or sensing learners. They also have to take into account two other categories of learners, the reflective one who is usually quite calm or the kinesthetic one who has to be active while learning.

You will have to be able to catch each person's individuality and adapt accordingly. Being an open and adaptable person is not enough, you will still have to learn methods such as differentiation, balancing the various learning needs. You will also face students suffering from all kinds of particularities such as hyperactivity, ADHD (attention-deficit hyperactivity disorder), depression related to the teenage years and many others. All the paradoxes that exist in our disciplines, in our students, and in ourselves will have to be encompassed and this takes a special kind of person.

Added to the fact of having to adapt to their young or teenage audience, teachers have to adapt to their whole school environment. They must understand the community their students are part of, they must follow school administration policy and get on with staff. In this complex equation one must add students' parents with whom they need to collaborate too. And sometimes, dealing with parents can be more challenging than dealing with their offspring!

Being empathic and caring about people.

This is another aspect of emotional intelligence that is so necessary for being a teacher. Showing empathy and concern is much more important than people seem to think. I wrote a whole chapter in my previous book in which I explain why empathy and caring are so important. I shall just paraphrase the chapter in a few paragraphs here. Nel Noddings, an American feminist and philosopher followed up the notion of

Care which was first developed by Milton Mayeroff in his book On Caring in 1971. Noddings says that care is an asymmetric relationship in which the care-giver is sensitive to the needs of a recipient and tries to respond to him or her. There is a movement towards the other and towards the other's interests. The best example is the relationship between mother and child but it can also be applied to others like teacher/student, doctor/patient, trainer/trainee for example.

When interviewed on what characterizes a good teacher, students almost always say that they don't care much about the amount of knowledge the teacher has as long as he or she shows some concern and care towards them.

Willing to accept criticism.

Teachers must be ready to question themselves at all times and constantly improve their methods. Once again this goes much further than a simple yearly assessment on performance that is carried out in the corporate world. Teachers are assessed each and every day by their audience. They will receive verbal and non-verbal feedback on their performance on a daily basis and this is what destroys bad teachers in the end. They can't take the pressure. Remember you will be performing in front of an average of twenty youngsters who are sharp-eyed and who do not miss a thing: what you say, how you say it and even what you are wearing. My favourite remark, that makes me laugh each time I think about it, was made by a fourth-year student who was not listening to a word I was saying, he was just staring at my shoes. He then looked up at me and said, "Mrs Broda, ballerines in the 21st century? Seriously?" I could not help but burst out laughing. I answered that I was flattered that he thought that I looked young enough to be wearing Nikes, Doc Martins or Converses!

Another more serious remark has stayed in my mind until now. It was when I was going through a tough time in my personal life. One student said to me, "It's no good piling on concealer, we can all see you haven't been feeling great lately." I am thankful for all of my students' remarks, they have always acted on me as a wakeup call.

On a more serious note, the slightest mistake on the part of teachers will be scrutinized. Teachers who don't accept self-analysis fail to reach a fulfilling career. We spend our time assessing our students, we must accept the fact that they assess us too sometimes. We are not perfect and will never be, we can just try to improve day after day. Some teachers fail to see criticism as constructive they just take it at heart and see the destructive aspect of it. These constitute the second category of people who experience burnout. They set a hierarchy scale that is illusionary. They refuse to see that they are human and being human means learning from our mistakes.

Accepting failure or drawbacks.

This means teachers need to have the maturity to recognise that sometimes teaching goes terribly wrong. All teachers have experienced a moment when nothing works, and the class is just lifeless or in other cases totally uncontrollable. Teaching is similar to some kind of occult art that is practically impossible to master completely. It cannot be codified or reduced to an algorithm that is guaranteed to work each times says Parker J Palmer. All good teachers know that there are some good teaching days and some bad ones and these happen even when we prepare everything so carefully that we are surprised that things just don't go the way we wanted them to. I once had such an unpredictable group of students that I used to joke that I started thinking of what I was going to do in my course as I was putting the key in the door to open the class. Although this is obviously an exaggeration, I honestly had to feel the atmosphere within the classroom to know what was going to work on that day. Sometimes the best lessons are ones that are instinctive with no preparation. How come?

The secret is that there is an alchemy, something indiscernible about what goes on between all the human entities that compose a class. And that energy force which is the combination of all the individual energies can sometimes be destructive. It is as though you have the wood and the lighter but somehow you can't light the fire. There is no use feeling guilty about it, more often than not, it is neither the fault of the teacher nor of the students, it is just the connection between both entities that is not there. But while a good teacher is affected by a lesson that goes wrong, a bad one just doesn't care because he or she knows they will still get their salary. When this happens to us, we must try to understand it by analyzing in more depth the complexity of teaching and try to be able to get it right next time around, yet accepting the fact that sometimes we will get it wrong whatever we do.

Having a sense of humour.

Teachers who have an innate sense of humour start out their career with a huge advantage. They are able to dedramatize whatever is thrown at them. Sometimes students' remarks can be hurtful but if you take them on the funny side, things go smoothly instantly. On the other hand, I can say that there is not one teaching day in which I do not find something to smile about in my students. I usually bring home the best stories and tell my family and we all laugh together. Seeing what is endearing in others is part and parcel of this profession.

It works both ways because students love humorous teachers. Comic relief is always needed in a lesson. It bonds the teacher to the students, it alleviates tensions, erases problems and fluidifies the lesson. I use it all the time and students love it.

But beyond the fun factor, a sense of humour can be an effective way to engage students and activate learning. It creates a comfortable learning environment. When teachers share a laugh or a smile with students, they help students feel more comfortable and open to learning. This brings enthusiasm, positive feelings, and optimism to the classroom. It also fires up the brain. During her research on learning and humour, educator and researcher Mary Kay Morrison looked at brain scans that showed high levels of activity in multiple areas of the brain when humour was used in conversation and instruction. We're finding humour actually lights up more of the brain than many other functions in a classroom, says Morrison, author of Using Humour to Maximize Learning. She adds: In other words, if you're listening just auditorily in a classroom, one small part of the brain lights up, but humour maximizes learning and strengthens memories.

Adapting to exterior circumstances.

Not only do teachers have to adapt to a great variety of students and of learning skills but they have to constantly adapt to exterior circumstances too. These happen all the time and every day. If the OHP doesn't work, if the computer breaks down, if you lose your class key, if a student comes in late, if a student is unruly, if the fire alarm goes off, if two students start fighting etc. A teacher must perform on several levels all the time, meaning that if you are working plan A, you must always have a plan B and C ready in the back of your mind. And when you are dealing with one difficult student, you must juggle with the rest of the class simultaneously.

Multitasking.

This derives from the previous ability and is part and parcel of the job. It is commonly said that women can multitask better than men. Well, if this is true, men teachers had better develop the feminine side of their brain fast because teaching means doing several things at the same time, all the time!

Some people flourish in a job situation where they know exactly what is expected of them. Yet for many, the thought of repeating the same task for hours every day sounds deeply unpleasant. If you are the type of person who avoids getting stuck in a rut, teaching may be just right for you because it is a job with built-in variety, as you work through new units, teach new topics, and work with different children each year.

Self-control

Being calm and patient is another must. To follow up the previous point, when unexpected things happen, you have to be calm enough to deal with the situation. This takes a little practice, but in my opinion, it is basically an innate quality.

Teachers who overreact or get angry fast or are too nervous have difficulty in holding the job. Being patient is paramount. Not only to deal with the situation but by doing so you are also being, at the same time, a model for the other students watching you. You have a role to play and you have an audience. You will be working with teenagers who are on another level altogether. Little by little you will understand that ultimately, they will not adapt to you, you must adapt to them and for this you need a lot of patience, self-control and philosophy.

Optimism

Having a positive outlook on life, being optimistic and showing trust in youth is paramount. In my previous book, I talk at length about the fact that we have to have faith in our teenagers, understand them, love them, respect what they are going through and basically support them in every way. Every day, I hear teachers complaining about their students and I find that it all adds oil to fire. Instead of criticising them we should be more positive and encouraging. They all have potential although it is sometimes not the one we are looking for, at a given moment. We often concentrate on the three skills, languages, maths and science but forget to look at all the other skills that are equally important like creativity, originality or imagination.

Being imaginative.

Being a teacher is about finding a way to get students to learn, and sometimes these new learning methods can be risky. This demands a lot of imagination to innovate and keep the class motivated. Good teachers have new ideas all the time, they want to experiment with original ways of transmitting knowledge. They follow self-development courses throughout their career to go on learning and perfecting their art. Both teachers and learners should use imagination in learning because imagination and knowledge support each other in the quest for authentic learning.

Imagination can be defined as the faculty of forming new ideas or concepts of external objects not present to the senses. And knowledge encompasses the skills we acquire through experience or education. Our imagination is organic, it changes and grows as our knowledge grows. Then imagination which has been fed with knowledge spurs us on to new experiences and knowledge. This cycle of discovery and learning is what we are looking for in education. It is not only to be adapted to the student but also to the teacher. An imaginative student will state opinions rather than just give correct answers. In the same way an imaginative teacher should also take risks, adapt to the situations and to the changing needs of the students, experimenting with new approaches and new methods.

But is it possible to teach students how to be imaginative? I would say that you cannot actually teach it but you can model it. If the teacher is really passionate about a new idea and shows it is possible to think out of the box, the students will feel free to follow that creative path too.

This reminds me of Dead Poets Society, the 1989 American drama film directed by Peter Weir, written by Tom Schuman and starring Robin Williams. Set in 1959 at the fictional elite conservative Vermont boarding school called

Welton Academy, it tells the story of an English teacher, Mr Keating who inspires his students through his teaching of poetry. At some point, he tells all his students to stand on their tables to show them that our perception of things depends a great deal on our point of view. He shows them that reality can be seen very differently according to our perspective. It is the same reality, but seen differently. This approach helps some of his students to deal with their problems in a different way and to have a new outlook on life.

So imagination can create a unique bond between the teacher and the students. By going further in discovery and experiences, they can ask themselves, what if? Although teachers need to follow certain standards in their curriculum, they have the opportunity to inject their own personality into their job, and this is great.

Teamworking.

Imagination has shown how it can create teamwork between a teacher and his class. Enjoying working with colleagues is also a kind of teamwork that is important. Sharing teaching manuals or methods, opinions, experiences, problems and solutions. A teacher who keeps to himself is usually an unhappy one. You have to accept staff support which should be around you.

At the beginning of my career, I was quite isolated, I didn't know many other colleagues and kept to myself. I thought it was impolite to ask for help or to share documents, tests or evaluation sheets. Little by little, I opened up and shared my work with others. This was liberating. Now we all form a huge knitted group, made of teachers of a variety of subjects. We help and inspire each other continually. It is what I call "teacher's room bliss": being surrounded by people who think and function just like you and with whom sharing experiences is always inspiring.

Leadership.

Students need someone to guide them, to be in charge, and to set the tone in class. Leadership is needed but it has to be built on natural charisma and not on blind authority. This is an issue I feel very strongly about. I might shock a few traditional teachers here, but according to me, charisma is far more important than authority. Authority will help you manage a group and obtain what you want by force. Leadership built on natural charisma will make your audience want to do what you ask them to. I might be the least authoritative teacher you will ever meet, but believe me, I can make any student do what I want him or her to do because I know how to induce into him or her the will of doing something without being ordered to do so. It has to do with positive emotions which trigger a psychological mechanism called mood contagion.

Emotional or mood contagion is the ability to influence the emotions and behaviors of others, either directly or indirectly. Emotional contagion is used as a strategy in work settings and relationships. Our brain helps us to read other's emotions to show us how appropriate our responses should be. For me, emotional contagion works both ways. I as a teacher should be able with my personal disposition to induce students to follow my instructions in order to achieve some task, but on the other hand I should be aware of their emotional state too. If a student is visibly not focused and cannot get down to work, instead of punishing him or her, I try to understand what is going on with questions like: you don't look as though you are in a good mood for work today, what's going on? More often than not, this breaks the ice and the students will tell you why they cannot focus. In which case I leave them alone and more often than not, after a few minutes they start working because they feel understood. They see that I respect their feelings and more often than not they do make the effort of working to please me in return. If they choose not to, it is okay too. This is where emotional intelligence is needed.

But if leadership is induced by charisma, one has to realise that charisma also needs time to flourish. Some people are too shy to let their real personality shine through, they think that they have to hold back and have a neutral behaviour in front of a class. With time and experience you learn that being yourself will liberate you and build bridges between you and the students. That is when your charisma will show.

At the beginning of my teaching years, I was like a robot in front of my class. I thought you had to be standardized. An experience proved that I was wrong. Indeed, part of our training was to be filmed in class by our assessor. When I saw myself on the screen, I didn't even recognize myself. "Is that me?" I asked.

"It looks like you but it is not you. You are hiding who you are, you are taking on a 'fake teacher' role" he said. "You are doing this to protect yourself. If you want to become a good teacher, you have to release your inner self. Let the students see who you really are otherwise there will always be a distance between you and them and you won't be able to communicate properly. You have charisma but you are too shy to let it shine through."

Exploring and exposing your true-self and teaching from that standpoint creates an authentic relationship with students. Everything then becomes much easier.

As mentioned before, I have never been an authoritative person, it just does not fit with my personality and very honestly, I can say that I am quite allergic to it. In my opinion, when someone exercises excessive or badly placed authority this immediately creates an atmosphere of tension which freezes any positive energy. Being authoritative is like being out of a circle and giving orders to people who are inside it, being charismatic is being within the circle with the others and obtaining them do something you want. The difference is that here you are part and parcel of what is happening. There is a flow to and from you and the students. With authority it is one way only. I mention the limits of authority in my previous book, based on a survey that was carried out in a professional school. The bottom line of the research showed that the apprentices needed to feel that the educator showed both empathy and concern. Many of them complained about the lack of exchange, indifference and detachment on the part of their teachers as well as their misplaced authority.

Communicative and organizational skills.

You will be taught lots of hard skills in your teacher training course, two of which I would like to mention because they are related to some of the above-mentioned aptitudes. They concern communication and organisation. But how to talk in front of an audience, how to make a good presentation, how to use technology also largely depend on the pre-existence of more social skills. Keeping in mind that even the best methods and the most up-to-date equipment are of no use if in the hands of teachers who don't have the basic human requirements needed to communicate. I shall develop this aspect in the chapter on digital teaching.

Similarly, prioritizing and organizing are skills that can be learned too. I often joke about the fact that you don't have to be a Virgo to become a good teacher although their organised mind does give them a huge advantage. Little by little you will learn that if you are not organised in your lesson plan, your marking and general administration, life will soon become hectic. Prioritizing is important not to get overwhelmed. There are some periods during the school year when you feel that you are unable to get on top of things and that you are drowning. Lessons, tests, exams and marking, all come at once. A good teacher usually has a bag full of highlighters and a well organised diary. It is more to do with having an overview of a situation, seeing things from above, being able to see the big picture as it were. Some people are too limited in their scope, they like to take things one day at a time and find it very difficult to plan out a school year. So if you are naturally organised, this will be of great help.

If you have read all these prerequisites carefully, you will have understood that the ingredients for being a good teacher are numerous and can be categorized in three domains: Firstly, they touch cognitive areas like methodology, didactics, knowledge of subject matter which you will learn during your training. Secondly, they also have to do with emotional intelligence, that is the way you interact with others, what kind of person you are, how you feel when transmitting knowledge and the way others feel when learning from you. Finally, there is a third level which is less tangible and more mysterious and which is how we apprehend life on a larger scale, a kind of feeling that animates people who love doing their job. A quest for a more universal connection, something that nourishes one's soul and satisfies the inner-self. All this is part and parcel of good teaching.

If all of the above resonate with you there is yet one more thing to consider before being sure that teaching is for you. And this is time, because time is needed to anchor your beliefs. As mentioned before, skills and passions are organic. They grow with time. You have to experience teaching for a while to see if the activity coincides with who you are. You must also work hard to learn how to improve your teaching skills and how to handle your audience It is a long-term process, there are no short cuts.

So the best advice I can give you is to start and make your way in the profession and see how it grows on you. Even if your first incentive was triggered by the wrong motivations such as the number of holidays, flexible schedules or anything related to external factors, get experience and you will soon find out if this activity makes you happy or not. Maybe at the end, the answer will be: I thought teaching was for me but it isn't. In which case things can be redirected and usually very easily as explained earlier on with the example of the person who shifted from teacher to social assistant. She wanted to help children but eventually realised that she didn't want to transmit knowledge to a group of them. She was more comfortable helping young people solve their problems individually and therefore achieved a masters in psychology.

On the contrary, refusing to see the evidence and continuing in a career that you know is not good for you is always worse for social professions. Not liking to type on a computer all day long is bad and can be frustrating but the computer will not complain about your lack of investment. If you don't like being a teacher your students will feel it in no time and the alchemy between you and them will deteriorate year after year, resulting into frustration, rebellion and ultimately depression or burnout for the teacher. The students will get along fine because the relationship will only have lasted one year, but the teacher will have to hold on with each new school year bringing another load of dissatisfied youths.

Another aspect that Ken Robinson mentions is self-realization. In teaching this has to be considered also from the student's point of view. A good teacher will be able to spot out what a student is good at and will value that aspect. So not only do teachers have to be sure they are doing the job which coincides with their inner self, but they should help students find their own path and discover their own abilities and passions. This is related to the qualities mentioned above concerning care, empathy and interest in others. I shall come back to this subject later when taking about the future of school.

CHAPTER 4
REFLECTION ON SCHOOL METHODS AND ANALYSIS OF PISA GRADING

Education has always been a field that has been plowed over and over and still is. One school reform is followed by another. The educational system has too often been targeted towards a future driven by business interests and therefore missing its core aim. But learning under digital conditions is a whole new deal which is going to uncover an alternative conception of the future.

In my opinion the multitude of reforms which become obsolete one after the other is precisely the symptom that we are looking the wrong way and that's why we come up with solutions that seem better at the time but are never really hundred per cent satisfying. It seems obvious to me that recurrent cosmetic changes are not going to make the substantial difference educators are looking for. They indicate that we are on the wrong path. Things have to be thought out on a different level, out of the box.

So the questions to ask is first of all, what is it we are aiming at? Are we doing things right and is our focus where it should be?

When thinking about education on a large scale, what if the ever growing progress of technologies is precisely what is going to give us the answer? Technology is making us focus on something else. The answer may be right in front of our eyes. By going forward scientifically, we are going to be more critical about our past methods which remained for most of them, inadequate. Despite the numerous reforms, most of them well intentioned, if you think about it, teaching one same lesson to a large group of different individuals has little to no sense at all.

So although pessimistic people see in technological advance the end of the value of teaching and a regression of the teacher's role, I think on the contrary that it can serve education if managed properly. Technological changes have to be mastered as well as behavioral changes in students whose profiles are radically changing too. What if all this is finally pointing towards what was clear from the beginning? That each student is different and unique and needs to learn his or her own way.

All the people who have analyzed the subject of the future of education in depth are unanimous: education technology will be personalized. Transmission of knowledge will be characterised by the fact that teachers will be able to adapt their teaching to the individual and to new profiles, thanks to all the new connected tools. Artificial intelligence and big data are part of the innovative technologies that will redefine pedagogical approaches completely. Things are changing in a big way and more importantly, for the best. As the technical aspect of teaching is changing drastically, teachers have to adapt, as always. But all the aptitudes mentioned in the previous chapter will still be needed even if the infrastructure of a class is going to be very different.

I often compare teachers to chameleons, they have to change colours according to each situation as fast as possible not to be eaten up by their predator. In the teacher's case, the danger is becoming a has-been teacher who is not following fast moving trends. Teaching at school or university in the twenty-first century entails connecting with an increasingly highly technologically skilled public. More than ever, academics have to be competitive and up to it.

So we no longer have time to fiddle with small methodological changes because we are in the midst of a huge and daunting transformation that we can hardly control but which, at the same time, is fantastically challenging. So how can the future of education be better than what we have now?

First of all, we are currently teaching students who will be engaged in professions we don't even know will exist. Secondly, we are stuck in focusing on basic branches like maths, languages and science whereas reality shows us every day that we should open up to more creative skills. Most schools seem to be formatting youth into some employable person at the cost of making young people discover who they are and what they are good at. It is much too often putting aside skills like creativity and the arts in general. Ken Robinson develops this notion in his book Creativity in Schools.

WHAT PISA TEACHES US

I find the acronym PISA very adequate, it is a tower that is relentlessly falling on its side. By showing the shortcomings of standardization teaching today with a special focus on evaluations such as Pisa I will show how the future may bring something all good educators were consciously or unconsciously waiting for. Although many see education of the twenty-first century as dangerous and limiting, it might be exactly what we need. The challenge of twenty-first century education is to give everybody a chance to succeed and the tools we are going to have may well be the right ones.

Pisa stands for: Programme for International Student Assessment According to the Wikipedia definition, it is: a worldwide study by the Organisation for Economic Co-operation and Development (OECD) in member and non-member nations intended to valuate educational systems by measuring fifteen-year-old school pupils' scholastic performance on mathematics, science and reading. It was first performed in 2000 and then repeated every three years. Its aim is to provide comparable data with a view to enabling countries to improve their education policies and outcomes. It measures problem solving and cognition.

Policy-makers in most participating countries see PISA as an important indicator of system performance and as a valid and reliable instrument for international benchmarking. Pisa has both advantages and disadvantages. On the one hand data from international standardized assessments can be useful in research on causal factors within or across education systems. The databases generated by large scale international assessments have made it possible to carry out inventories and comparisons of education systems on an unprecedented scale. One of the conclusions is that although culture may not be the reason for high results, countries do play a massive part in this. The results show that which country you study in, if you're from a disadvantaged background, massively affects your results. Therefore, PISA's ability to compare countries' education is extremely important as it highlights how in some countries it is easier to overcome your disadvantages. It also shows that everyone has the potential to do well in life, but that a country and its education system can make all the difference.

On the other hand, PISA has its detractors like Ken Robinson who said: The PISA league tables have become like the Eurovision song contest of education. We all know what the Eurovision song contest has done for the quality of popular music — not very much.

I totally agree with this statement because the main disadvantage is that many of the skills that students need and excel in are not measurable by PISA. As Johan Brand founder of 'Kahoot!' explains, PISA is supposed to create a level playing field, but actually what it's doing is creating an average that's not relevant to anyone.'

Standardized testing doesn't necessarily help unless you are lucky enough for that type of examination to compliment the way your brain works. However, this style of assessment does little to inspire creativity and individualization.

Therefore, the problem with PISA is that it focuses on a very narrow conception of education, it is all about testing literacy, numeracy and science which are obviously very important but they ignore the depths of talents that students really have. Education cannot be limited to being good at reading or maths or science. PISA is an indicator of whether an education system is good or not but it seems obvious that the future is based on broader concepts. We need creativity, social sciences, arts and music —— things that PISA doesn't measure at all.

The other revelation made by PISA is that those who do well in science don't necessarily want to become scientists and vice versa. The discrepancy between ability and aspiration is something that has to be taken seriously. So many children do not realise their dreams because they are never assessed on what matters for them. PISA is all about competition, and in my opinion, competition should not play any part in education, it should be replaced by collaboration.

I remember that when I was a pupil in a French catholic school, we were ranked first, second or third of the class. All the other children were lost in a group of average to not so good. This was humiliating for students and totally destructive. First of the class in what? In a subject a student may not even like? Why not find what the worst one in the class is capable of, or likes to learn? A cluster of Asiatic countries which regularly have good PISA results, like Singapore and Hong Kong, introduce competition in their education at a very early age. But interestingly enough there is another country that is often top of the lead and that is Finland. However, Finland had not made the choice of strict competition and like other northern countries they don't believe in standardized testing. On the contrary it has an innovative education plan where every child receives a good education with each school performing on the same high level. They have a broad curriculum and they promote collaboration instead of competition. I will come back to Finland in the last chapter, showing the country's philosophy on education and choice of methods.

If we look at the case of Singapore performing first out of seventy-two countries in the 2015 PISA grading, let us also point out the downside of this victory. The OECD has detected above-average levels of anxiety among Singaporean students about their schoolwork compared to other countries. And an official report from Singapore points in the same direction. People in the government are realising the problem like

Education Minister Ong Ye who announced changes in Parliament. He declared: "We need to balance the joy of learning with the rigor of education. Indeed, Singapore has put education at the heart of its development since independence in 1965 and has lost all perspective in wanting so badly to make their youth educated."

Singapore's students also rank third in the world for the time spent doing homework at home, averaging 9.4 hours a week according to the OECD. Society doesn't want to afford the luxury of taking things slowly says psychologist Daniel Koh of the Insights Mind Centre. Children are being forced to grow up too fast, without the necessary foundation and reasoning power to reassure themselves, says Koh. In order to reduce school pressure, the Singapore authorities intend to abolish certain examinations in primary and secondary schools and change the school curriculum that is considered too rigid.

The island state is not an isolated case in Asia. School work is cited by the Hong Kong Centre for Infant Mortality Studies as one of the main causes of teenage suicide. In 2017, Japan recorded its highest rate of adolescent suicides in thirty years, with a peak on 1st September — the start of the school year.

The UK also focuses a lot on school competition — which school beats the others and how do you get your kids into that school. The focus should shift from opening grammar schools and putting schools in competition with each other — to how to accommodate and lift up those who are falling behind within each individual school.

The situation in the United States with the programme No Child Left Behind showed similar flaws. The 2002 NCLB Act of Congress supported standards-based education reform based on the premise that setting high standards and establishing measurable goals could improve individual outcomes in education. The Act required States to develop assessments in basic skills. To receive federal school funding, states had to give these assessments to all students at select grade levels.

The act did not assert a national achievement standard because each state developed its own standards. NCLB expanded the federal role in public education through further emphasis on annual testing, annual academic progress, report cards, and teacher qualifications, as well as significant changes in funding. The bill passed in the Congress with bipartisan support. By 2015, bipartisan criticism had accumulated so much that Congress stripped away the national features of No Child Left Behind. Its replacement, Every Student Succeeds Act (ESSA) turned the remnants over to the States.

One of the problems is that outside influences often affect students' performance and this is not taken into account when assessing them. Students who struggle to take tests may perform well using another method of learning such as project-based learning. Sometimes, factors such as home life can also affect test performance too, so the fact of basing performance on one test only is not reliable and it inaccurately measures student success overall.

In conclusion, not only PISA, but other educational assessments point out something that is very clear. Education is not about pushing all the students into reaching an identical goal but more to develop their inner potential and this can be done with personalized education. This may be coming our way thanks to both ITC and AI. The following chapter will attempt at showing to which extent the role of the teacher is going to change accordingly.

CHAPTER 5.
HOW ITC AND AI ARE CHANGING THE
TEACHER'S ROLE

INTRODUCTION

In the twenty-first century we will learn and teach differently for sure. Globalization will establish new rules different from those which have been dictated by the industrial society. Artificial intelligence will reinvent education which is bound to be more personalized and new technologies will accompany the learning path of pupils and students.

This new century still has the same challenges that education has always had, which is to give everybody a chance to succeed, but this time around it is both Artificial Intelligence coupled with Information and Technology Communication that might be the precise tools that will finally achieve this.

Let us start with a powerful announcement, made by Benjamin Vedrenne Cloquet, partner at IBIS Capital and co-founder of Edtechxglobal. He claims that:

"Focusing education on how we learn as opposed to what, is the key. Lifelong learning and informal learning will soon become the two pillars of a new form of learning architecture. An architecture that harnesses the social reach of the internet, the ubiquity of artificial intelligence, on demand education resources, and the use of neurosciences to deliver rapidly and effectively bite size personalized learning throughout our lifetime."

He goes on:

"In this new world, the new teachers may take two forms. One could be software mobile companions or bots helping and encouraging humans to constantly upskill and earn Nano degrees in a race against accelerated skills obsolescence and job displacement. Another role could be the one of a 'brain farmer', moving away from managing and transmitting knowledge to using the fields of learning science to seed motivation for learning and creativity."

One thing is sure, education will change in the next ten years much more than it has in the previous two thousand years!

To better understand what Benjamin is saying, let us define the word bot. Bots are software applications that are programmed to do certain tasks. They are automated, which means they run according to their instructions without a human user needing to start them up. Bots often imitate or replace a human user's behaviour. Typically, they do repetitive tasks and they can do them much faster than human users could. It is a little frightening to think that teachers are going to be so dehumanized.

However, as education is a systemic subject which involves many actors, not only must we concentrate on 'how' instead of 'what' but in order to benefit from the contributions of artificial intelligence and cognitive sciences, we must also focus on the long-term objectives, and not only on the means. The final goal being to enable children to find a satisfying and fulfilling place in society. So we have to look at how these new technologies will address their individual academic abilities and various talents, as explained in the previous chapters.

In many countries, like all professionals, teachers are already seeing their activity turned upside down by digital technology. On the one hand, tablets and intelligent software have started invading classrooms while teachers are still having to teach subjects and skills that may well be obsolete tomorrow. Indeed, sixty-five percent of today's school children will be engaged in jobs that have not yet been invented. This poses the question of how can pupils and students be trained for jobs that do not yet exist and how must the teaching profession have to tailor their practice to be more relevant?

Schools and universities around the world are currently investing heavily in educational software and equipment but will also have to set a huge budget on training courses to help teachers benefit from these advances. Education professionals have to learn how to use all this new technology and also reflect on how differently they have to transmit knowledge.

Added to the technological progress, the understanding of the human brain and learning mechanisms has made considerable progress over the last two decades too. The combination of all these findings is crucial for individualizing training and ensuring a high level of education for all. Before looking at the practical aspect of these changes, I would like to mention one of the biggest challenges in my opinion of ITC applied to education, and that is time management.

5.1 TIME MANAGEMENT

Although teachers are used to taking part of their job home with them, so to speak, they are going to do this on a whole new level in the future. Indeed, they will be working overtime by being constantly connected to their administration, to their colleagues and to their pupils or students. Very few of them will be able to disconnect because school is going to invade their everyday life. Being able to delimit their private sphere is going to be close to impossible because of the open line of communication between all the various entities. The line between school and personal life is blurred by these technologies that serve as a link between the two worlds. Nowadays the classroom and the outside world merge into one vast space for work and study beyond the walls of the classroom and beyond teaching time. Paradoxically teachers will benefit from technology but will also be, to a certain degree, slaves to this new educational network.

We are already exchanging emails, SMS and WhatsApp messages all the time. But now students, colleagues and administration staff are gradually stepping in and are becoming part of this huge communication web. If I compare my involvement now and ten years ago, the change is already tremendous. I occasionally had a call in the evening on my landline from a student who apologised for disturbing me but basically all the exchanges happened during class. Now all this has changed with numerous online communities linking everybody all the time.

So although it is commonly thought that ITC is a time gainer, it also involves a lot of hours and effort to be mastered correctly and the input on the part of the teachers is much greater than when it was just them, their lesson and their students. So although technology enables us in some cases to troubleshoot faster and save time, we definitely lose the peace and quiet we had when we were disconnected.

This overflow is obviously due to massive data exchange of information and documents but also to increasing online assessing. Even in traditional lessons, students do not really take notes any more, most of them just take a photo of what is put on the OHP or they can receive the content of their courses directly onto their accounts. Most university courses are now online for the students to be able to follow them, even if they miss the lecture given live. This means that all the courses have to be carefully planned ahead and put into user friendly e-form.

All these changes have a direct effect on the nature of the relationship between the student and the teacher because they are in constant virtual contact. Modern technology creates a personalization of teaching that was previously unattainable. It is more like a cooperation between two people, although students might sometimes be far ahead of their teachers in technological matters. Having been using them from an early age, they are more at ease with the tools that most teachers are trying to adapt to, and adaptation takes time. Moreover, the time needed to acquire good working methods is still largely underestimated in cognitive terms. This is perhaps the most important pitfall generated by the illusion that ICTs will solve everything.

5.2 TEACHER'S ROLE IN THE USE OF ICT AND AI

So one can legitimately wonder about the role of teachers in dematerialized, digital or even automated classrooms and lecture halls. Do they still have a role to play and are they still useful in a world of unlimited access to knowledge and personalized learning? The answer is undeniably yes and this is what I shall demonstrate.

The use of information and communication technology (ICT) gives students access to a huge range of documentation made possible through the internet. This plethora of information will have many consequences. The first one is that it changes the way teachers manage their subject. For example, a literature teacher knows that students have access to sites like Teachit or Spark Notes, meaning that they may be ahead of them in acquiring basic knowledge related to a novel or a play.

Summaries, main themes, character descriptions and so on are all within easy reach with a simple click. Very often students read about all the characters before even having started to read the book. They adapt their knowledge to the reading experience instead of doing the opposite and discovering what the characters are like by analyzing the text. The obvious danger here is that students want to go faster, and get relevant information the easy way. But studying literature should be exactly the opposite. The excitement comes from the fact of discovering little by little what the author is trying to say by reading chapter after chapter, building up links and connections, just like a puzzle, putting all the pieces together one by one to get the whole picture in the end.

Every year I see students at exams reciting information taken from the internet about a novel but not having found this information themselves by true analysis. Their production sounds false, it is artificial and formatted. Even worse, many students do not even read the books any more, they just Google the author and his work.

Here the role of the teacher is to educate their public, explaining how to go about an analysis and developing their critical mind. Do they agree with what they read on the internet, why or why not? How can they justify what they are saying with quotes from the text?

The second consequence of the flood of information which students have access to, is that a significant proportion of them have difficulty accessing the most relevant online resources. These new technical resources can even be a real obstacle for them to acquiring complex cognitive processes. They run the risk of getting lost in a maze of tools and documents of unequal quality and this is where the teacher's role is also paramount. The teachers have to intervene as coaches in the learning of their students, who are trying to evolve with almost total autonomy. But this autonomy will have to be redirected towards relating and interacting efficiently with information that is easily available but which has no kind of order or filter whatsoever.

The question that this raises, is that if students must build their skills and acquire necessary knowledge, which skills and knowledge are we really talking about? How does one guide the students and what are the practical drawbacks? How long will the learning of the tool be in comparison to the subject matter itself? The forced autonomy of the student and the apparent generalization of access to electronic resources give a false impression of immediate accessibility which leads to underestimating the actual time needed to master the resources and especially, to master the process of reflection.

Indeed, some students put a huge amount of effort finding data on a specific subject but their own end product is disproportionately disappointing. Students are going to have to be more proactive and actors in their learning. If teachers need time to adapt to ITC, students need it too. It is not just a question of being handed our tablets. We have to talk about information competency. How does one get relevant information in a world in which there is too much of it?

Here teachers are far from being just virtual tutors for students, they have a role, much like the one they always had only the subject matter is different. They need to teach how to prioritize and criticize first-hand information. This competence has a name: cognitive ergonomics. This is the answer for a successful integration of information and communication technology.

5.3 COGNITIVE ERGONOMICS

The official definition of cognitive ergonomics is: a scientific discipline that studies, evaluates and designs tasks, jobs products, environments and systems and how they intersect with humans and their cognitive abilities. It is defined by The International Ergonomics Association as concerned with mental processes, such as perception, memory, reasoning, and motor response, as they affect interactions among humans and other elements of a system.

The objective of cognitive ergonomics is ultimately the optimization of human well-being and system performance. It comprises elements such as mental workload, decision making, skilled performance, human reliability, work stress and training as these may relate to human-system design. In our case we shall speak of HCI, that is human-computer interaction, both by the teacher and the student.

Cognitive ergonomy is supposed to help the teacher prepare and give a course, the management of pedagogical resources as well as work assessment. So if student usability is the main objective, it starts with the teacher usability first. Again, getting to be proficient in this domain demands time investment on the part of the teacher and the student.

Cognitive ergonomics applied to the teacher must facilitate the preparation and delivery of the course, the management of teaching resources and the correction of work. However, not only the time needed to master new software or platforms cannot be underestimated but teachers also need pedagogical assistance to make sure that they are maximizing the tool.

Others may go further developing a new tool and this involves programming which can be considered as a nightmare for non-scientific minded teachers. This is when a good synergy between teachers within a school is useful so that the end production is not only effective but manageable by everybody.

Cognitive ergonomics applied to the students must facilitate access to a course and knowledge of the platforms but also must teach them how to use all the technology available in an intelligent and productive way. Educators have the challenge of teaching their students to make sense of this hyper rich information and to make the most of it effectively. This leads us to information literacy.

5.4 INFORMATION LITERACY

In this global information age, information literacy, which is also called information competency, is essential for success, both in college and in everyday life. It is the use of judgment in determining good quality sources of information. Applied to our subject, it is the mental processing of information by students and the usability of all that technology puts in their hands. This emphasizes the importance of pedagogical strategies which involve active engagement on the part of teachers or professors in transmitting core concepts in whatever field they teach. It also shows the importance of helping students in acquiring a set of abilities to locate, evaluate and use effectively the needed information.

Although information literacy looks like a new term in the higher education lexicon, it is far from being a new concept. Indeed, it has been around for a long time in libraries where librarians have always been involved in teaching the effective use of information resources under the labels, library instruction, bibliographic instruction and library skills. This role is going to be largely taken over by teachers for their respective subjects.

The term information skills was first introduced in 1974 by Paul Zurkowski to refer to people who are able to solve their information problems by using relevant information sources and applying relevant technology. But the concept of information literacy was introduced with the establishment in 1989 of the American Library Association's Presidential Committee on Information Literacy. They determined that information literacy is a critical skill for student success in this information age.

The American Library Association has listed five key skills that an information literate person must attain. It differs from the traditional library instruction in that it involves a collaborative effort between librarians, computer science, and other classroom faculties. It also focuses on the learner, rather than on the teacher, and on teaching lifelong skills rather than on teaching a specific function of various library resources. According to the Association, an information literate person:

-Determines the nature and extent of the information

needed.

-Accesses needed information effectively and efficiently.

-Evaluates information and its sources critically and incorporates selected information into his or her knowledge base and value system.

-Individually or as a member of a group, uses information effectively to accomplish a specific purpose.

-Understands many of the economic, legal, and social issues surrounding the use of information and accesses and uses information ethically and legally.

Let us compare this with the definition of information competency adopted by the California Community Colleges Academic Senate:

"Information competency is the ability to find, evaluate, use, and communicate information in all its various formats. It combines aspects of library literacy, research methods, and technological literacy.

"Information competency includes consideration of the ethical and legal implications of information and requires the application of both critical thinking and communication skills."

This same document lists the skills that students must be able to demonstrate in an integrated process in order to be considered information competent. He or she:

-States a research question, problem, or issue.

-Determines information requirements in various disciplines for the research questions, problems, or issues.

-Uses information technology tools to locate and retrieve relevant information.

-Organizes information.

-Analyses and evaluate information.

-Communicates using a variety of information technologies.

-Understands the ethical and legal issues surrounding information and information technology.

-Applies the skills gained in information competency to enable lifelong learning.

In conclusion we can say that centering teaching on the learners does not mean leaving them to their own devices in the self-construction of their knowledge, but rather seeking to understand with empathy the dangers encountered on the cognitive level and providing them with the means to acquire skills as well as knowledge. Many of the aptitudes mentioned in the first chapter are also important here. Empathy, patience, interest in others etc.

So here the role of the professors seems clear. As experts in their field, they should be able to mark out the useful documentation in the abundance of information on a particular subject. Their other role is to get students to ask themselves about the most relevant work strategies, provided that they are put in a situation where they can practise and try them out. This is where an important element has to be taken into account even more so when students are dealing with ITC, which very often implies multitasking. This new element is concentration.

5.5 MULTITASKING AND CONCENTRATION

One of the biggest challenges is getting students to focus on using electronics for learning and not for social networking. And for this they need to concentrate. Concentration refers to the mental effort you direct towards whatever you are working on or learning at a precise moment. It is sometimes confused with attention span which refers to the length of time you can concentrate on something. This is well known by teachers who deal with ADHD students who are usually characterized by a persistent pattern of inattention, hyperactivity and impulsivity. Concentration difficulties can also be linked to simple things like sleep deprivation, underlying mental or physical health conditions such as brain injuries, neurological conditions, depression, anxiety and sometimes vision problems. What is relevant for our subject is when the difficulty to concentrate is linked to major cognitive functions such as memory and attention.

The first element which might defer concentration is the nature of the document one is working on. Do we focus as well while reading on a screen as when those same words are on a printed page? Apparently, we do not, precisely because of all the distraction that is going on when the text is read from a computer, a tablet or a mobile phone. Many surveys show that people say that they can concentrate more and feel like the content sticks in their mind better when they get the information from a paper document.

Fortunately, technology which is the very cause of the multitasking threat can sometimes provide a solution to problem it has generated. More and more internet explorers do provide distraction free reading modes which help a bit. Programs, such as Instapaper, Pocket, Readability, Clearlyand or Evernote offer to declutter the screen of unwanted distractions. The browser Safari also provides a convenient reading mode. One can download Adblock which works on most web pages. Despite the decluttering, concentration is proven to be more difficult when reading information from screen.

The second element is multitasking. Whether in class or out of class, ITC lead students into a world where they are inclined to do many things simultaneously. Writing a text, searching for a reference on the Web, finding interesting information by chance and sharing it with contacts, replying to an instant message, etc. All these things can be done at the same time, but is it still possible to concentrate in these conditions? And if it is difficult to limit this kind of distraction in a classroom, how can one monitor students' attention when they are remote learning?

In class, teachers all know how difficult it is to keep the students' attention when working whether with computers or not. But out of class, things are uncontrollable. Most of them will tend to adopt multitasking behaviors, and are distracted by e-mail, web browsing or texting. Constant on-screen notifications, pop-ups and visual alerts will impair students' concentration. Considering all these temptations one may wonder what happens to the motivation to "build one's own knowledge" under these conditions.

This is where the teacher has to inspire students showing them that concentration is something that they must acquire and practice not only because they have to, but ultimately because they want to. By understanding how it works they can choose to be proficient or not.

Multiple studies have been made on what happens during the learning process when multitasking. We also know more about how memory works and what effects distraction has on it. The first thing to understand is that when your brain is stimulated to perform many things at a time, you have the false impression of being capable of doing them all. People feel more productive and believe that multitasking is the only way they cope in a world of information overload but the reality is that the brain is incapable of actually focusing on many things at the same time, so production is weaker. In reality, your brain is madly switching from one thing to the next, often losing data in the process. So in fact you are not multitasking efficiently, you are just task switching.

The other effect of multitasking is that it is addictive. When we are doing one thing only, we feel we are wasting time and we could be doing other things as well. When attention is split, each task gets less focus. In fact, if the tasks you are doing are relatively unimportant and do not require undivided attention to complete, multitasking can help to get more done. But if you have an important job or one that requires particular attention or care, the only way to achieve it satisfactorily is to stay focused on it.

In his 2009 study: Cognitive control in media multitaskers, Clifford I Nass, Professor of Psychology at Stanford University says: People who multitask often have a high level of confidence in their abilities, but we know that these people are actually less successful than most in cognitive tasks or in activities which involve memory.

This illusion of competence is one of the things that most concerns researchers studying attention, cognition and learning. This is much more serious than what used to happen in traditional classes when a student sometimes got distracted or lost in his or her thoughts. A student today who jumps quickly from reading to writing a text message then to taking notes and back to reading social media notifications may well feel, at the end of the day, in control and proud of having managed to do everything at once, but the reality is that he or she has absorbed much less of the lessons than someone who was concentrating on what was going on from the beginning to the end of each one.

The first studies on multitasking and memory date back to 1890. The undeniable conclusions today are the following: researchers seem to have reached the consensus that there is an overlap of two otherwise distinct neural systems: the one which controls attention, activated when you read a document for example; and the other one which controls attention from a stimulus, for example when you turn around when the doorbell rings, or someone enters the room. What is important to know is that however intelligent you are, beyond a fairly low level of multitasking, everyone's performance breaks down. There is a limit of the number of activities one can do at the same time.

This is what Etienne Koechlin, director of The Frontal Lobe Functions Group, and his colleague Sylvain Charron demonstrated when writing about the cognitive cost of such distractions back in 2010.

He came to the conclusion that tasks are less well performed when multiplied. Each half of the brain focuses on a specific task when trying to do two things at once. This division of labour may explain why it is so difficult for us to multitask.

After multiple experiences using magnetic resonance imaging techniques, he observed that the activity in the left frontal lobe corresponds to the main task (action A) and the activity in the right lobe corresponds to the secondary task (action B). The brain is able to control switching between its two hemispheres when performing two functions at once, but lacks precision when a third task is added.

Dr. Etienne Koechlin says: "You can cook and talk on the

phone at the same time, but you can't really perform a third task like trying to read a newspaper. If you perform three or more tasks, you lose track of one of them."

Dr. Koechlin also believes this brain behaviour may explain why people make "irrational decisions" when they have more than two choices. "From my point of view, irrational decision making is intimately linked to this division of labour between the two hemispheres of the brain that allows the brain to follow the thread of performing two tasks or to choose between two options, but no more," he says.

He continues: "Our results are likely to provide an explanation for the fact that it is easier for people to make the right choice when there are two options than when there are several." This would explain why we are more likely to make irrational decisions when it comes to choosing from a long list of items.

We all know how dangerous it is to drive and look at your phone at the same time. Here we have the added function of what is called "channeling", that is that when you are reading a text on your screen your mind is oblivious of what else is going on around you. Although both are terribly reckless, statistically, it is more dangerous to drive and text than drive while under the influence of alcohol or cannabis.

So although scientists seem to agree on the dangers of multitasking as far as concentration is concerned, they do not agree on the way to describe the relationship between attention and work memory. There is an unsolved question and that is: is it a weak attention system which causes a weak work memory or does this work backward to? Why do some people seem to be able to keep their attention on a single task while others are unable to? And how much work memory is stored in our students' brains when they finish an activity? Can we count on what they have learnt or is the information going to be erased in a very short laps of time?

Michael J. Kane, Professor of Psychology at the University of North Carolina says, "The disparity in working memory capacity accounts for about half of the disparity in individual reasoning and interpretation. There is no consensus on what makes this relationship. But there are a number of mechanisms that seem to come into play."

One of these seems intentional, Kane says, "The idea that my colleagues and I are putting forward is that part of the explanation for the differences in individuals' memory capacity is that people with very high working memory capacity can simply control their attention better. They make an effort to prevent distractions from interfering with their work."

Here we have to make the distinction between fluid intelligence versus crystallized intelligence.

Fluid intelligence is the ability to use logic and solve problems in new or novel situations without reference to pre-existing knowledge. Crystallized intelligence is the ability to use knowledge that was previously acquired through education and experience. The first one declines with age and the second can be maintained or improved.

The theory was first proposed by psychologist Raymond B. Cattell and developed further with John Horn.

These two categories of intelligence can obviously work together but what makes fluid intelligence so precious is that when you encounter a new subject you use your brain to understand the material through logic and analysis.

It has also been proved that strong attention skills produce stronger fluid intelligence. Strong attention can produce projective and creative reasoning. Attention and distraction are intertwined not only in reasoning and memory, but also in the encoding of information in long-term memory. Therefore, distraction during learning can be very harmful, even if the distraction does not seem to interfere with students' immediate performance in their tasks.

Karin Foerde neuroscientist at Columbia University, and colleagues, argue that when subjects are distracted, they learn the rules through the semi-conscious system of habit memory, and when they are not distracted, they memorize them through what is called the declarative memory system.

Obviously teachers want students to be able to extrapolate and make analogies. This is not possible with a semi-conscious system of habit memory.

This explains why if you want to make sure a student has understood a grammar point you explained, you can ask him or her to explain it in detail and with his or her own examples to another student. This will show straight away if the assimilation of information that was provided is effective or not. Very often, students think they understand an explanation merely because they were listening to it, but their minds were not really fully concentrating either because of multitasking or because the subject itself was not motivating enough for them at that point in time.

A student who understands a grammar rule because he was fully concentrating, will not only be able to reproduce what he has learnt but will have acquired the additional skill of extrapolating, maybe making similes with other languages or other grammar rules. This process needs concentration and cannot be done if multitasking gets in the way.

Taken to the extreme, Professor David E Meyer, Professor of Psychology at Michigan University tried to give lessons to his students without any computer, tablet, or phone. Students were not even allowed to take notes on a piece of paper. The aim of his experiment was to capture their attention one hundred percent. He wanted their attention to be focused solely on him and on what he was saying.

But does multitasking have any advantages then? The answer is yes, it does have some very good sides to it. It is even taken into account when recruiting staff as a positive attribute. Recruiters are looking for extremely competent people who can achieve lots of tasks simultaneously because they want to save time, and time is money. Little do we know that multitasking does also have some cognitive benefits of its own.

N. Katherine Hayles, English Professor at the University of California at Los Angeles has written a very interesting article, 'Hyper and Deep Attention: The Generational Divide in Cognitive Modes'. She argues in a series of essays that multitasking actually develops other competences in people. She says that the new multimedia world generates "hyper-attention" that is different from, but not necessarily worse than, "attention" in the traditional sense.

Her hypothesis is that we are in a generational shift which has to be acknowledged for what it is and we must not try to change it, but rather adapt to it. This change in cognitive styles is a real challenge for education at all levels. She compares deep attention, that is the ability to concentrate on one subject for a long time, ignoring side stimuli and the preference of one single information stream to hyper attention which prefers a high level of stimuli, multiple information streams and constant switching focus. In a media-rich environment, she believes, young brains are increasingly making the conceptual connection between a wide variety of fields. Like if one's efficiency was maximized by getting things done in parallel with each other.

Her conclusion is that this new way of working and studying is a reality and instead of resisting it we have to, in some cases, adapt our educational strategies to meet it. This means that our students are not just multitasking because it is a trend, they have actually got used to doing it, they like it and are addicted to it.

This hyper attention is also what is developed in people who are frequent video game players. I once followed a seminar on the effects of video games on youngsters and was amazed by all the positives that this activity could bring. If, and only if, time management is under severe control, playing video games develops a list of skills like reflexes, reactivity, motricity and coordination. It can even improve vision. If the amount of time spent on the device is too long, the effects become negative. Moreover, video games seem to be responsible for the development of multitasking capability in terms of attention, hand-eye coordination and visual and spatial problem solving.

Let us come back to the informational or digital overflow that students are experiencing today. This cognitive overweight has been called infobesity. Ongoing research is done to try to understand how the brain copes with all the information. If we are submerged with new data all the time and if it is at hand permanently, one could wonder if memorizing information is really as necessary as before. This is where the "just in case" is replaced by "just in time". We are witnessing a new learning style in which answers come at a rapid pace. We are also experiencing a certain frightening obsolescence of knowledge and of skills. So how can we act efficiently in the learning process of our students in a world that is getting more and more complex? As said earlier, our frames of references are changing and we have to try to adapt.

I would like to mention two concepts that will help us find answers. The first one is transformative learning and the second one is mindfulness.

5.6 TRANSFORMATIVE LEARNING.

If you are interested in education that radically changes the way people think and the way people feel, it is worth exploring transformative learning theory. It was developed to help educators understand the nature of significant and powerful learning that changes the learner into profound long-lasting ways.

Jack Mesirow is at the origin of the concept of transformative learning, developed in 1975. His theory is that everyone has a set of meaning perspectives that they develop according to their upbringing and experiences. These are taken for granted in the way we see ourselves and the world. When people encounter new knowledge, they tend to add this to their existing way of seeing things. New knowledge doesn't transform the way we look at things it just builds on it, it adds to what we call our existing meaning schemes. Transformative learning happens when we encounter new knowledge or experiences that don't fit into our preconceived meaning perspectives. Mesirow calls these disorienting dilemmas. These can shake our way of seeing things so in order to manage this new knowledge and set of experiences we have to reformulate our meaning perspectives, we have to make them more inclusive, we have to change our assumption and reformulate our beliefs. This can be difficult because it involves critical reflection.

Mesirow theory has developed into a comprehensive and complex description of how learners construe, validate, and reformulate the meaning of their experience. His complex theory can be simplified and adapted to our subject.

I have shown that the teacher's role is to guide, to coach and to accompany students on their learning path. Teachers have to adapt to the new reality which is a world of easily accessible data overflow. Not only do they have to tailor their practice to this new reality but they have to help students have a reflexive analysis of their behaviour by developing their autonomous thinking.

Transformative learning can be associated to Meaning Making and Critical Thinking. These terms are related to the constructivist approach of famous educators like Jean Piaget or Maria Montessori for whom meaning is constructed from knowledge. Mezirow starts from that point of view to question it.

Mezirow shows that there is a difference between transmissional, transactional and transformational education. In the first, knowledge is transmitted from teacher to student. In transactional education, it is recognised that the student has valuable experiences, and learns best through experience, inquiry, critical thinking and interaction with other learners. Learning is considered transformative if it involves a fundamental questioning or reordering of how one thinks or acts. In other words, reflection alone does not result in transformative learning unless the process involves a critical reflection, a recognition and analysis of taken-for-granted assumptions.

Therefore, students have to be made aware of their way of functioning so that they can appreciate both the pros and the cons of their learning behaviors.

What I find interesting in transformational learning is that encapsulates most of the elements that I have pointed out earlier. Indeed, the role of the educator is to provide an opportunity by assisting learners in becoming aware and critical of their assumptions but also of the tools they use. We are back to digital literacy. Educators must also provide learners practice in recognising frames of reference, redefining problems from different perspectives. Here we are back to the originality that made Mr Keating so special. The goal is to create a community of learners who are "united in an experience of trying to make meaning of their life experience", or understanding how they function in this digital world. Promoting discovery can be implemented through group projects as it is done in the Flipped Classroom. The teacher must also build trust and care to facilitate the development of sensitive relationships among learners, two skills that were introduced earlier on too.

Not only do the learners have to go through this process of transformation, teachers also have to do it. We come back to the fact that there is not hierarchy between teachers and learners, both are in a kind of discovery journey.

New teachers often find expectations ambiguous, and they lack the self-awareness and understanding to navigate the educational environment. Whether young or experienced, they should all go through the process of questioning their role and practice. This was expressed as one of the basic pre-requisites at the beginning of my analysis when talking about accepting criticism, advice and collaboration with peers.

According to Mezirow, learners must create norms within the classroom that include civility, respect, and responsibility for helping one another learn. Learners must welcome diversity within the learning environment and aim for collaboration. This is part and parcel of the digital citizenship that I shall develop later on, but also refers to one of the skills that is so important that is adaptability.

Finally, transformative learning has two components that at times seem to be in conflict: the cognitive, rational, and objective and the intuitive, imaginative, and subjective. Both play an important role in learning. This is exactly what I highlighted in the prerequisites when talking about the third element, the alchemy between students and the teacher. Something that is felt and experienced but that cannot be rationally described.

So is multitasking and dealing with a flow of constant information just destroying reasoning capacities in our students and is it totally detrimental to learning? Apparently, the answer is no. It is merely a new aspect of the learning process that we have to live with, adapt to and monitor. And only a human being can do this, artificial intelligence cannot bridge this gap — at least not yet. This will require a radical change in the mindset of teachers. In other words, teachers should not ask themselves what the child's problem is, but rather what they need to do differently in order to be successful in reaching out to them. This requires teachers to search tirelessly for best practice and to continually refine their work.

If we have to accept this new generation's way of functioning and try to make the best out of it, the answer may be to counteract the negatives with new ways of thinking and learning in order to find a constructive balance.

Transformational learning is based on the defining condition of being a human which is that we have to understand the meaning and the functioning of our learning experience. There is another tool which can help us and our students adapt to the changing world of massive data, and this is Mindfulness.

5.7 MINDFULNESS

Mindfulness Meditation Practises (MMPs) are a subgroup of meditation practices which are receiving growing attention and can offer multiple benefits. They can increase attention, focus, memory, concentration and other cognitive abilities. They help to maintain a moment-by-moment awareness of our thoughts, feelings, bodily sensations, and surrounding environment. Its motto is being alive and knowing it.

Based on Buddhist meditation, a non-religious practice of mindfulness has entered the mainstream in recent years, in part through the work of Jon Kabat-Zinn and his Mindfulness-Based Stress Reduction (MBSR) program, which he launched at the University of Massachusetts Medical School in 1979. Since that time, physical and mental health benefits of mindfulness in general have been proved and lots of programs have been adapted for schools, prisons, hospitals and other structures.

Mindfulness is becoming more and more present in educational domains and is making its way slowly but surely in classrooms and online. It offers a counterbalance of calm and control to the constant agitation caused by the flow of incessant information that over-stimulates the brain of our students.

We are not far from John Dewey's view that learning is life — not a preparation for it. Just like transformational learning, mindfulness also requires authenticity, a commitment to focus on the here and now, and awareness of feelings and emotions within the learning setting. The greatest gift of mindfulness is that it teaches us to choose what we want to focus on. It has been shown that practising mindfulness alters the structure and function of the brain, which makes it easier for us to learn and memorize. It is all about learning to use our attention in an effective way and being more mindful about where you place your attention. When you take on each task with full awareness, you make significant progress on your projects, you start appreciating your time, stop wasting it on things that do not serve you, and dramatically reduce your stress level. With practice, students start to notice where their attention is going and they try to deal with the distractions by bringing their focus back to the task at hand.

Sessions of mindfulness are offered to teachers and students in the school in which I work. More and more collagues take a few minutes before starting a lesson to help students shut their eyes and focus calmly on what they are going to do during the lesson. It is a practice that is widely spread in teacher training courses. The idea is not to try to turn back time but on the contrary to accompany students in today's multitasking life by, first of all, making them realise what is happening when they do several things at once and showing them how to adopt periods of deep concentration, willfully refusing external stimuli.

Just as our students have to be guided and informed about

information literacy, concentration and ways to improve their collaboration with technology, they also have to be informed of other pitfalls such as cyber bullying, cyber-crime and other similar dangers. This leads us to another problem which is part and parcel of the digital age which is digital citizenship.

5.8 DIGITAL CITIZENSHIP

Approximately one in three users of the internet in the world are under the age of eighteen, therefore it seems obvious that educators have yet another challenge. They have to support children and young people in a world filled with social media showing them how to be responsible citizens and building resilience to potential dangers like cyber bullying or child predators.

Digital literacy is often equated with digital citizenship but there are distinctions. Here it is not only about teaching young people how to select information that is widely available but it is also to show them how not to be a victim of it. Digital citizenship refers to the ability to engage positively, critically and competently in the digital environment. This includes being able to draw up effective communication, to create content and to engage in social participation while being respectful of human rights and dignity.

Digital Citizenship Education (DCE) has two aspects to it. Firstly, it is the empowerment of children through education to use technology in a responsible fashion and to protect themselves from any misuse or threat

Secondly, it seeks to ensure that those who are not "digital natives" or do not have opportunities to become digital citizens, or digizens, are not marginalized in future society.

With the development of relatively inexpensive technology, the digital gap is more likely to be a gap in skills required to make advanced use of the technology than access to technology per se.

In a number of countries, schools are introducing Digital Citizenship Education to encourage young people to develop their online proficiency, engagement and creativity as well as an awareness of the legal implications of their online activity such as copyright or plagiarism.

There are many resources for teaching these concepts, and a great place to start is the International Society for Technology in Education (ISTE). Their comprehensive standards focus on the skills and qualities students should have in order to be successful in the digital world. ISTE also teamed up with Google and developed an online digital citizenship game called Interland. It educates kids about digital citizenship in interactive ways. Students learn how to be good digital citizens as well as how to combat hackers, phishers, over sharers, and bullies.

If a school is going to allow and/or encourage the use of digital devices in the classroom, then teachers also need proper support in terms of training, professional development, and curriculum. They can start with curriculum and PD resources such as those provided by Common Sense Media, but in order to fully utilize them, teachers need time to plan and collaborate. Digital devices should only be used when there are specific goals in mind, focusing on student safety, digital citizenship, critical thinking, collaboration, advancement, and equity.

Anne Collier is a journalist who has followed youth Internet safety and citizenship for nearly twenty years. She gave a famous Ted Talk a few years ago in Geneva (2016), a town which is a symbol of children's rights. She said, rightly so, that citizen literacy has to be learnt just as digital literacy or social literacy (also called social competence or emotional intelligence). Also, digital safety filter devices are not always the solution as far as teenagers are concerned. They are a good solution for very young internet users but teenagers are at an age when they need to make their own choices and just blocking out dangerous content will not solve the problem because they will go and get access to it somewhere else, either on their phone or a friend's computer. What is needed is their collaboration and their own judgment to learn and decide what is right or wrong to be aware of potential dangers and become responsible, ethical digital citizens.

The teacher's and parent's role of keeping communication open with teenagers for sensitive issues including cyber security is developed at length in my previous book on adolescence.

CHAPTER 6.
COURSE MANAGEMENT SYSTEMS

The concept of the classroom as an individual space is evolving. Tablets in the classroom, total rethinking of the class' architectural layout and new digital tools are all part and parcel of the many changes that have already occurred.

In this chapter I shall show how the digital environment is already improving the efficiency of the learning process inside and outside the classroom. I shall start with some learning platforms and digital practices that are already very much in use transforming classical classrooms into virtual ones with e-learning and remote teaching. Educational software platforms designed to support teaching, research and collaboration are also known as Course Management Systems (CMS), Learning Management Systems (LMS) or Virtual Learning Environments (VLE).

We use the term Asynchronous Learning when referring to forms of education, instruction, and learning that do not occur in the same place or at the same time. It uses resources that facilitate information sharing outside the constraints of time and place among a network of people.

In many instances, well-constructed asynchronous learning is based on a student-centered approach that emphasizes the importance of peer-to-peer interactions. Course Management Systems have been developed to support online interaction, allowing users to organise discussions, post and reply to messages, and upload and access multimedia. These asynchronous forms of communication are sometimes supplemented with synchronous components, including text and voice chats, telephone conversations and videoconferencing.

The main thing to remember is that technology, whatever its shape or form, must always be purposeful when applied to education. What is boring on paper will be boring on an iPad. Digital activities must not only be skill based which can sometimes be discouraging for the student, they also have to be project based to stimulate their creativity and self-confidence.

Digital technologies provide solutions to many problems, among others, overcrowded classes, rooms that are not always suitable and absenteeism. Differently from the conventional school environment we have more and more educational institutions choosing smart classrooms, with an interactive board which replaces the black board or OHPs and the students each having a device which enables them to share all their data not only with the teacher and but with other students. Computer based programmes enable teachers to innovate and students to benefit from one-to-one teaching, rapid feedback and constructive individualized support. Examinations and general assessment are also widely computerized which creates more flexibility.

This new concept of the open classroom goes even further, leading to global connection. Thanks to broadband technology, teachers in one school can reach out to students in other schools. Interactive videoconferencing systems also allow them to work in cooperation with their peers in other countries. One can organise a virtual school trip in a museum in Rome or in an Animal Reserve in South Africa. The possibilities are endless.

But although the quick pace of technological innovation has brought a multitude of opportunities to the world of education, it is also a great challenge for teachers and for students to adapt as mentioned in the previous chapter. Yet there is another issue that arises from technology-based forms of education which is a challenge that schools themselves have to face. Indeed, acquiring technology that quickly becomes obsolete is a huge investment that can be a deterrent for some schools. Some of them are being left behind because of it.

To solve this problem, many schools use the BYOD method, that is Bring Your Own Device. The BYOD trend started in the corporate world in which employees were asked to use their own technological devices instead of the ones provided by the firms. Adapted to the educational world, BYOD means that classroom digital devices would not only be purchased by the school, students would also have the option to use their own smartphones, tablets and computers to complete class projects or access learning resources while in class.

This concept has both benefits and a few drawbacks. Educators in favour of BYOD feel that it promotes greater participation and enthusiasm in the classroom. Schools that want to remain ahead of the curve in terms of innovation find that the BYOD program carries a positive image. Supporters also say that using laptops, tablets, and cellphones in the classroom can keep students engaged, because technology is what they know and feel comfortable with. On the other hand, opponents of this system worry that the BYOD program will increase the already significant divide between students from high and lower-income families. It could widen the gap because the investment of families in technology varies greatly. Some economically disadvantaged students do not even have a computer at home. Some schools have the means to address the digital divide so that all of their students have access to technology and can improve their technological skills. Meanwhile, other schools still struggle with their computer-to-student ratio and lack the means to ensure a balance between all classmates. Despite these problems which could be addressed by schools lending devices to some needy students with more government help or solutions provided by private initiatives, it seems that the prevalence of student-owned devices in the classroom is definitely continuing to grow, helping more and more students to access technology within their school.

Before showing a panorama of some IT tools that are already widely in use inside and outside the classroom, I would like to say a word about a special mode of teaching called The Flipped Classroom. It is more a philosophy than a method which makes great use of the digital technology that is going to be presented.

6.1 THE FLIPPED CLASSROOM

Also called the inverted class, the flipped classroom did not come from any predetermined will to implement a new teaching method, it happened by chance. It all began in 2007. Jonathan Bergmann and Aaron Sams, two American teachers, wanted to make videos available to certain students who were too often absent, allowing them to follow the courses at a distance, whenever they wanted. The project was a success and even exceeded the initial objectives, attracting the interest of hundreds of thousands of people around the world.

With the flipped classroom, it is both in and out of the classroom that technology is going to be used to rethink teaching and learning modes. It is based on blended learning where students are introduced to content at home and then practice working through it at school. This is the reverse of the more common practice of introducing a new concept at school then assigning homework and projects to be completed by the students at home. The benefit of this system is that time spent in class is more an interaction between people than a group listening to one person speak. The flipped classroom is more and more popular in many countries because it values the individuality and personality of each student, the importance of which I have shown in the previous chapters.

The lessons made available to students can come from a variety of online sources that students will watch at home at their own rhythm. Teachers can even create their own content. When the students enter the class, they all have something to share about the subject and can bring in their own contribution, ideas and questions. Here technology is used and shared within the group, giving the students a lot of initiative. The teacher and the students are in collaboration mode, and the lesson is more an informal workshop in which everyone can participate. The inverted class puts an end to the supposedly boring lecture, favoring the "gifted" students and putting the others aside. Teachers are not the only ones who have the power. Students also have something to show, demonstrate or teach. Some parts of such lessons are a little like, 'genius hours' when students choose their project instead of having one imposed on them and therefore, they can select what to learn.

6.2 IT RESOURCES

Although some software is not free and entails some sort of financial contribution, there are many open-source ones which is an obvious plus in a school setting. You have the freedom to run the software, study it, redistribute it, change it or integrate it in your environment.

My survey of what is available is by no means exhaustive as the quantity of material is huge. New software is being produced non-stop and older ones are constantly upgraded. As I cannot name them all, I shall try to give a kind of overall view of some of the educational material which is available. It includes course management systems (CMS) i.e., platforms to bring classes online and other software that teachers and students can use independently. In my list I have prioritized systems that I have worked with or that are used in my close environment. I have added as often as possible first-hand comments made by friends or colleagues.

The Interactive White board.

Let us start with what has replaced the good old blackboard and overhead projector: The IWB, commonly known as smart board or interactive white board. This is a large interactive display surface. It is used in a variety of settings including classrooms and university auditoriums. We see them more and more in broadcasting studios for the news or weather forecast, they are also omnipresent in corporate board rooms for which they were designed and manufactured in the first place.

The IWB can either be a standalone touchscreen computer

used independently to perform tasks and operations, or a connectable apparatus used as a touchpad to control computers from a projector.

A device driver is usually installed on the attached computer so that the interactive whiteboard can act as a human input device (HID), like a mouse. The computer's video output is connected to a digital projector so that images may be projected on the interactive whiteboard surface. The user then calibrates the whiteboard image by matching the position of the projected image in reference to the whiteboard using a pointer as necessary. After this, the pointer or other device may be used to activate programs, buttons and menus from the whiteboard itself, just as one would ordinarily do with a mouse. If text input is required, user can invoke an on-screen keyboard or even handwriting recognition so that it is not necessary to go to the computer keyboard to enter a text. Teachers can conduct a class almost exclusively from the whiteboard.

In addition, most IWBs are supplied with software that provides tools and features specifically designed to maximize interaction opportunities. These generally include the ability to create virtual versions of paper flipcharts, pen and highlighter options, and possibly even virtual rulers, protractors, and compasses — instruments that would be used in traditional classroom teaching.

Teachers can use the IWB according to their level of knowledge. Usually, they start using it as a didactic support or visual support, then later as an interactive device or a stimulator and finally as an enhanced interactive tool, when they produce content.

One of the browser-based digital whiteboard software

which is free and easy, is called Open Board.

Open Board

This free open-source cross-platform teaching software for interactive whiteboard was designed primarily for use in schools and universities. It can be used both with interactive whiteboards or in a dual-screen setup with a pen-tablet display and a beamer. It was forked from Open-Sankoré 2.0, which was itself based on Uniboard, a software developed by the University of Lausanne. It was created with the help of a team of professors, specialists in communication, neuropsychologists and software developers to refocus the software on its original objective to implement the work of a teacher in a classroom and make it easier. From Switzerland it has been growing fast in Europe and in North America.

My school has made Open Board available to all teachers, giving them multiple possibilities to use various functions including writing, sketching, annotating on an uploaded document, recording sessions, integrating YouTube sequences and so on.

My colleagues find OpenBoard very user-friendly with various tools at the bottom of the screen such as pen, highlighter, laser pointer etc. At the upper edge you can adjust the colour, the line thickness and also advanced settings to the pages and the page background. On the right side you can display the library (images, sounds, videos…). Teachers also appreciate some mini applications like calculators, rulers, widgets for clocks or countdowns. There are also interactive applications such as Dice or Magic Box which can be individually configured and integrated into a lesson making it more fun and challenging for the students.

More experienced teachers use the podcast or screencast mode which allows them to record their lessons then have them published directly on YouTube or on their own network/intranet. The benefit of this is that it offers opportunities to make a lesson available to other people.

Moodle

Another well-known course management system is Moodle. It was originally developed by Martin Dougiamas an educator and computer scientist who lives in Perth, Australia. His aim was to help educators create online courses with a focus on interaction and collaborative construction of content. It is used for blended learning, distance education, flipped classroom and other e-learning projects in schools, universities and workplaces. Moodle allows for extending and tailoring learning environments using community-sourced plugins. Plugins are a flexible tool set, allowing users to extend the core features of the site.

The first version of Moodle was released in 2002 and is in continual evolution. For the first time user, Moodle seems more complicated but once it is mastered it offers numerous possibilities to make the teacher's work lighter. You learn progressively how to go further and further in all the things it offers. It also encourages the teachers to consider new pedagogical approaches which can transform and improve the teacher/student relationship. With customizable management features, it is used to create private websites with online courses for educators and trainers to achieve learning goals. As a learning platform Moodle can also enhance existing learning environments.

It has been chosen by the DIP (Département de l'Instruction Publique) in the canton of Geneva as a e-learning platform for schools. Teachers are encouraged to follow the training course which is divided into several levels to make it accessible to all ages. Swiss universities use it for their online courses and general student management. Among others the prestigious EPFL and UNIL in Lausanne and Geneva University use Moodle.

Colleagues I questioned about Moodle seemed to agree on several points. First of all, they appreciate the fact of being able to keep track of a course which is always accessible and which enables the absent students to catch up. This also facilitates revision for exams and provides reassurance to the students and to their parents. The second element which came out of my informal survey was that Moodle promotes collective corrections. Students can correct their peers' work, they can also add to the course or suggest new items. The third element is that teachers can collaborate in creating a course and one can substitute for the other easily. They all agreed that Moodle takes more time to master than other teaching platforms like Google classroom, but is more comprehensive.

University students, such as my own children, tell me that they particularly appreciate the forum that is included where they can exchange ideas and opinions with professors and assistants and the fact that they can follow all the courses online if it happens that they are not able to get to the University in time.

University teachers I have spoken to say that the fact that they have to prepare in advance and edit their courses is very demanding and makes them create better structured content.

They say that they collaborate more with other teachers just as students collaborate more with each other too.

Google Classroom is a learning environment system which was released in 2014 and is continually upgraded. My school actually used it during the Covid-19 pandemic when we only had twenty-four hours to switch from class teaching to online teaching. This says a lot about the user-friendliness of Google Classroom. It is really simple to use to start remote teaching and one can create a class group, distribute homework and grade assignments in a paperless way. The primary purpose is to streamline the process of sharing files between teachers and students.

Google Classroom combines Google Drive for assignment creation and distribution, Google Docs, Sheets and Slides for writing, Gmail for communication, and Google Calendar for scheduling. Students can be invited to join a class through a private code, or automatically imported from a school domain. Each class creates a separate folder in the respective user's Drive, where the student can submit work to be graded by a teacher. Mobile apps, let users take photos and attach to assignments, share files from other apps, and access information offline. Gmail also provides email options for teachers to send emails to one or more students in the Google Classroom interface. One teacher can also be 'invited' by a colleague to see what is being done within the virtual classroom.

If the teacher wants to communicate live with the students there is the application called Meet which is included in the options. This video meeting tool is very much like Skype, Zoom, Microsoft Teams, Teams and Google Hangouts which are all great platforms which offer group chats, screen sharing and video conferencing.

Some criticism has been made of Google Classroom, namely the lack of automatic quizzes and tests which are common features in other learning management systems and also the absence of privacy practices. It is nevertheless a very easy way for a teacher who is not very familiar with remote teaching to jump start a course.

Kahoot! is a learning platform that is currently being used by millions of users all over the world. Kahoot was founded in 2013 by Johan Brand, Jamie Brooker and Morten Versvik in a joint project with the Norwegian University of Science and Technology. They teamed up with Professor Alf Inge Wang and were later joined by Norwegian entrepreneur Åsmund Furuseth. The free game-based learning platform allows users to create, share and play fun learning games, and has become particularly popular in classrooms with the Bring Your Own Device programme. Kahoot! can be used to review students' knowledge, for formative evaluation or to break with traditional classroom activities. It can be applied to all subjects taught and also includes general knowledge quizzes. Not only do we have access to all the existing quizzes but teachers can make up their own, tailored to their course and subject.

Kahoot! was designed for social learning, with learners grouped around a common screen, such as an interactive whiteboard, projector or computer screen. The site can also be used via screen sharing tools such as Skype or Google Hangouts. It can also be accessed on mobiles. The gameplay is simple. All players log in using a generated game code displayed on the common screen and use a device to answer questions created by a teacher. These questions can be edited to award points. The points then appear in the ranking after each question. In September 2017, Kahoot launched a mobile application for homework.

Quizlet is another online study application that allows students to study information via learning tools and games. It was created by American Andrew Sutherland while he was studying for his French class to aid in memorizing words via flashcards. He then added various games and tests.

It is an easy way to practice and master whatever you are learning whether history, vocabulary, science or any other subject. The platform is updated regularly. Teachers can create their own classroom sets of flashcards or collaborate with other teachers, and students are motivated because the learning is more fun. As a memorization tool, Quizlet lets registered users create sets of terms and definition customized for their own needs. These sets of terms can then be studied under several study modes. Although the platform is implemented regularly, these are the main study modes which are most used. Quizlet has over three hundred million user-generated flashcard sets and more than fifty million active users.

My students love this learning website and use it very often to revise their vocabulary. There are many modes to choose from. From basic flash cards that you flip over for the answer, to gravity, where definitions scroll vertically down the screen and have to be validated before they reach the bottom; there are a lot of stimulating methods of learning. There are also always quick corrections so that the students can evaluate themselves. Also, some modes focus on long time memorization as opposed to short term memorization.

Quizlet is so easy to use that in my school we sometimes have the problem of students cheating during a vocabulary test. One click on their cellphone, and they have the answer they were looking for! Among its many additions, one dating back to 2017 introduced a new diagramming feature to help learners with subjects heavy on visuals like geography, anatomy and architecture and in 2020, Quizlet introduced night mode to all of its users.

Edmodo is a free and secure platform used by over thirty-eight million who exchange information in the field of education. It is a social medium a little like Facebook but adapted to school. The site allows schools to create a private communication network for sharing between teachers, parents and students. The site's interface is in English, but users can choose to translate the site into six languages by clicking on the flags at the bottom right; French, English, Spanish, Portuguese, Greek and German. Edmodo is therefore a space where teachers from around the world can exchange resources.

Edmodo's main pedagogical goal is to transform the classroom into a community through the power of social media. Its principle is based on the possibility of learning at any time and in any place. To do this, Edmodo offers teachers, students and parents a common space where they can contribute to the sharing of information, ideas and materials related to educational topics. Edmodo can also be used to introduce students to technology and to help improve communication through written language.

Edmodo is useful in several aspects. As far as the students are concerned, they can check their school grades and consult the list of homework to be done. They also have the possibility to write messages to their teachers and to the groups they belong to but not to their classmates directly. On the home page, a tool is available to help students manage their studies. There is a calendar where they can post the dates of assignments, exams, upcoming events or any other relevant information. Submission of assignments can also be done directly on Edmodo. Teacher comments on assignments are available to students. Many of them find motivation and curiosity thanks to this social network related to school.

As far as the teachers are concerned, they can create quizzes, launch polls and open discussion topics for their students. They can even create reward badges to increase class motivation. Thanks to the search engine, they can also share tips, tricks and teaching tools with other teachers in a virtual way.

One of my friends who teaches in London said this about Edmodo:

"I used Edmodo with a class from the South of France. Francophone students were required to express themselves in English, while British students could only express themselves in French. They worked on common themes, and exchanged multimedia productions, but also tourist brochures, for example. It was a great experience for everybody.

I not only use Edmodo in and out of the classroom with my pupils and with our partners abroad, but I also use it in training. It is an excellent tool for adult teacher training with colleagues within my country or with other countries in the world. It has broadened my teaching perspectives a great deal. Moreover, it is not difficult to use.

Microsoft Teams is another digital platform that is being chosen by numerous schools and universities because of the way it simplifies administrative school work and encourages collaboration between peers. This Course Management system makes it easy for educators and staff to create compliant Office documents using official and up-to-date templates and contents. The PHZH (Zurich University of Teacher Education) relies heavily on such templates and have found that Microsoft Teams is the answer for them. PH Zurich is training and inspiring the teachers of tomorrow by providing its nearly four thousand aspiring tutors with training, research, and support services to help them make a lasting impact on their students. The organization's eight hundred employees work with students, teachers, administrators, and researchers across Switzerland."

John Wilhelm, IT Lead at PH Zurich says:

"With all our templates, the problem was always updating them. With Office 365 and the officeatwork 365 web add-ins, rolling out new templates and updating them is so easy. Now it takes minutes to publish small changes and corrections." "For our users, everything just works, so that is a big productivity benefit."

Sakai is a platform used by some of the biggest American universities and hundreds of institutions mainly because they can be used simultaneously by millions of users. This LMS is also used in Canada, Europe, Asia, Africa and Australia. The Sakai software includes many of the features common to course management systems, including document distribution, a gradebook, discussion, live chat, assignment uploads and online testing.

In addition to the course management features, Sakai is intended as a collaborative tool for research and group projects. To support this function, Sakai includes the ability to change the settings of all the tools based on roles, changing what the system permits different users to do with each tool.

The core tools can be augmented with tools designed for a particular application of Sakai. Examples might include sites for collaborative projects, teaching and portfolios.

In Sakai, the content and tools used in courses or projects is organised into sites. Typically, a site corresponds to a course or a project. This is what allows Sakai to scale to hundreds of thousands of users. It is mainly used in universities. Major releases tend to be in spring or early summer, in order to allow institutions to upgrade before the new academic semester.

I asked an American colleague what he liked about Sakai. He said:

"I find Sakai a very powerful tool and as it is open-source, it offers the community members a license to change the structure to suit their needs. I particularly enjoy the discussion board and forums. The grade book is useful although it took me a bit of time and some help from colleagues to know how to navigate it. As for the negatives, it is not all that aesthetical and not mobile friendly.

Since I got this feedback, new major releases have continued to appear almost yearly. The main focus of development has been on incrementally improving the existing toolset and modernizing the look and feel, making it more suitable for mobile use."

Other useful software:

Chamilo is a free software e-learning and content management system aimed at improving access to education and knowledge globally. It is also used alongside Moodle by the University of Geneva.

Claroline enables hundreds of institutions worldwide (schools, universities, associations and other companies) to create and administer collaborative and educational platforms.

Ganesha created by Anema focuses on individualized courses. Unlike content management systems which are content-oriented, it organizes activities around the learner rather than around a course.

Ilias is one of the first Learning Management Systems used in universities, namely in Germany. The idea behind ILIAS is to offer a flexible environment for learning and working online with integrated tools. Ilias goes far beyond the idea of learning being confined to courses as a lot of other LMS do. Ilias can rather be seen as a type of library providing learning and working materials and contents at any location of the repository. This offers the possibility to an open knowledge platform where content might be made available for non-registered users too.

ATutor is another Open Source LMS, used to develop and manage online courses and easy to use to create and distribute interoperable learning content. ATutor is a free open-source web-based learning content management system developed to create and manage online courses easily. The project was first released in late 2002 by Greg Gay, after he conducted two studies and reached the conclusion that people with disabilities could not fully participate in an online course on any of the popular LMS available at the time.

Postclass wants to offer a collaborative tool to students and teachers. It sets up a kind of educational social network that allows these users to exchange after school hours. The application works on any medium and there is no need for an email address or a phone number. The idea is to offer a collaborative tool for students and teachers to easily pursue learning outside the classroom. It takes over from Facebook and other WhatsApp groups to offer a communication channel

111

adapted to education. The application also allows parents to communicate with each other about their children's activities and transmit official documents such as certificates or permission to leave the building.

In the same vein as Postclass, but focusing on the relationship between a student and his or her professor, Scoledge is a collaborative tool for institutions of higher learning. This "zero-mail" collaborative workspace allows professors to create their courses online, work with their students in real time and send them the resources they need while they learn.

Other software programmes can help create stimulating courses and can make a teacher's life easier. They are real time gainers once you know how to use them. They are great to create varied and stimulating classes, some of them using video and/or sound. Here is a small selection of the ones I have heard of from in my work environment, they are all open source. The first group are all aimed at recording, filming or designing.

Audacity is a digital audio editor and recording computer software application. Teachers often use it with Open Shot Video Editor. VLC media player is a portable and cross-platform media player and streaming media server. Gimp is a graphics editor used for image retouching and editing, free-form drawing, converting between different image formats, and more specialized tasks.

GCompris (French translation for I understand) is a high-quality educational software suite with a large number of activities for children aged two to ten years old. Some of the activities are games, but they have an educational purpose covering many different themes like reading, mathematics, science, geography, colours etc. All in all, GCompris offers more than one hundred activities and it evolves continually. It is a software you can adapt and improve according to your needs and even make available to children all over the world. The GCompris project is hosted and developed by the KDE Community.

GeoGebra is an interactive geometry, algebra, statistics and calculus application, intended for learning and teaching mathematics and science from primary school to university level.

Stellarium is a good tool for geography teachers, it is an open-source free-software planetarium, it renders a realistic projection of the night sky in real time.

Scratch is a free visual programming language and online community used by millions of children around the world. With Scratch, children can create their own interactive stories, then share and discuss their creations with one another. It was developed with the aim to help children ages eight and up to learn to think creatively, reason systematically and work collaboratively.

Gradekeeper might be good if teachers find it tedious to keep track of scores, attendance and all the information relevant to students' progress. This software records grades and other similar data.

QuizFaber is appreciated by teachers who have no previous knowledge of programming. It is an easy way to create true or false, multiple choice and matching quizzes that they may publish on the internet or send via email with just a few clicks.

What2Learn offers some relaxing yet useful computer games. From the website you can make fun interactive games like Hangman, Word Search or MCQs.

More creative teachers might be interested in using Picasa, a software developed by Google. It is an image editing tool that will allow you to edit the pictures you have stored in your PC so you may then use them in class on worksheets, games, coloring pages or flashcards. The albums you create can be shared with students.

Some of my colleagues love TestCommander, an invaluable tool for creating professional-looking online or printed tests. They are automatically graded with the results sent directly to the teacher. The tests can also be printed out on paper. The fact that it is free and easy to share makes it a popular software.

There are so many interesting innovations out there that I cannot mention them all. I just want to add one tool that can help both teachers and students to find out what is relevant in a long text. It is called Hilitext. This will highlight keywords making it easy to quickly scan a text for the needed information. I use it to teach students how to pin point crucial information in a text. I then give them an original text and ask them to highlight what they think is important and then compare both results.

6.3 MOOCS

Let us now have a look at the difference between closed and open online courses. There are other ways for learning a subject, whether mathematics, gardening or psychology and this is through Massive Open Online Classes (known as MOOCs). They include classes with various names like Master Classes or Webinars.

These online courses have democratized and delocalized knowledge that was previously only available in public and private schools. Although they also transmit knowledge, they are very different. The difference between these online courses and the learning management platforms that I have mentioned above is their very concept. Whereas an LMS is a platform for hosting a course, a MOOC for example is the course itself. A MOOC can be run on an LMS but does not have to be and similarly an LMS can be used to host a course that is not a MOOC.

The closed online course delivered by a school involves the distribution of modules or training courses on an LMS platform to a target audience. Learners can follow the course individually or collectively. The big difference brought by this mode of diffusion is the follow-up and interaction that can be done by the tutor through the private mailbox or in discussion threads. The resources put on, include interactive exercises and visual and auditory animations. The courses broadcast on the platform often require manual correction by the trainer.

The open online class is a course available and free and open to all, requiring no prior registration. It is very often distributed by training organisation and the validation of training courses does not necessarily require a certification. No teacher or trainer has to follow it up because the contents are usually exercises in the form of quizzes with an automatic response system.

The MOOCs initial target was to make knowledge available to the least educated and the most deprived in developing countries but unfortunately these online courses are mainly being followed in regions in which the population has a good or even very good level of education because they are mainly produced by 'Westerners'. There is also the problem of technical shortage in some areas which limits the access to knowledge. More generally a MOOC is a non-defined pedagogical format to teach or learn in an informal online way.

However, MOOCs have evolved and are made available from universities, even prestigious ones such as Stanford or Oxford. The online courses are monitored by a platform such as Coursea in the States, Futurelearn in the UK or France Université Numérique in France.

These new MOOCS can do obviously include communication between teacher and learner but also between learners.

Other Courses have been created along the same line, such as SPOCs, small online open courses and COOCs, Corporate Open Online Courses.

The Webinar (short for web-based seminar) is a presentation, lecture workshop or seminar that is transmitted over the web using video conferencing software. It has an interactive element to it. The presenter can give, receive and discuss information in real time. Today many webinars services offer live streaming options or the ability to record your webinar and publish on YouTube and other video services later.

Put simply, a webinar is an online seminar or presentation. Participants typically register using their email address and join in via a personalized link sent by the host. Inside the webinar, participants can see and hear the presenter, view slides and other media, ask questions, and sometimes answer polls. Webinars can be live or pre-recorded. Most often, webinars are free or at very minimal cost to the participants.

A Master Class is a course of development and sharing of experience given by an expert in a discipline e.g., in writing novels or painting portraits. Master classes online make it possible for anyone to learn from the best. Originally, Yanka Industries Inc. started doing business as MasterClass, an American online education platform on which students can access tutorials and lectures pre-recorded by experts in various fields. The concept for MasterClass was conceived by David Rogier and Aaron Rasmussen. The classes were typically not interactive. But now the term has been used more widely. Attendees of master classes typically already have pretty advanced knowledge in the subject area, but are looking to learn directly from you, as an expert. Typically, master classes are sold at a high price point because of the length of time and the depth of the material involved.

The other huge difference is that courses on LMS platforms are tailored for a specific public, like primary, secondary schools or universities. MOOCs, Webinars and other online courses are not always adapted to culture differences but they provide free online training and a multitude of diverse and varied resources. The learner has the freedom to stop the training at any time, unless it is a bachelor or master related course for which he has enrolled. Unlike closed courses that are attended by a defined number of learners, MOOCs leave the door open for a larger number of them.

Earlier on I spoke about new job descriptions that are making their way in everyday life. One of them is Digital Learning Manager. He or she is the person who is in charge of the organisation, management and implementation of MOOCs within an institution, be it educational or corporate. Being a digital manager means creating and implementing new learning design strategies, collaborating with instructional designers and program managers, implementing an adaptive learning approach that enables learners, whether students or employees to continuously learn in a personalized immersive and engaging manner. A digital learning manager must also be very much aware of all the up-to-date technology, software and apps.

CHAPTER 7
ARTIFICIAL INTELLIGENCE ADAPTED TO EDUCATION

Between promises, fantasies and fears, artificial intelligence is now a reality far beyond the "gimmick" stage. Machines that have human-like abilities to learn and make strategic decisions perform many tasks better than humans and this is just the beginning. We are creating machines that have abilities to learn and to make well thought out decisions.

Robots moving around the classroom to answer students' questions, helping them according to their personal abilities are already very much a reality and because of the more accurate feedback of the AI data, students are being helped with their individual needs inside and outside classroom walls. Thanks to this hyper personalization, AI systems are being used to develop a custom learning profile for each and every student

USA and China are the current leaders in this domain but artificial intelligence is growing exponentially all around the world. Within ten years, billions will be invested worldwide in numerous sectors including of course, education. All continents are doing their best to keep up with the machine learning curve. In Europe, the Coordinated Plan on Artificial Intelligence consists of adapting training programs to better prepare society for AI. The *Programme pour une Europe*

Numérique is planned to take place between 2021 and 2027. Many work groups from the OCDE are working on projects like the Working Group Digital Education. In Switzerland, where I teach, the two prestigious polytechnical schools in Lausanne and Zurich have already started working hard on the digital transformation in education with two initiatives: the Centre for Learning Sciences in Lausanne and The Initiative for Sciences of Learning in Zurich.

For countries like India or continents like Africa, the digital transformation is regarded as a game-changer. It represents an opportunity to boost economic growth and industrialization, reduce poverty, enhance education and improve people's lives in so far as e-learning can reach remote regions.

In this chapter I will mention the various areas for which AI is relevant in schools and universities and will enumerate several start-ups that are working on algorithms that are already transforming the way students learn. I will also give practical examples of AI based educational initiatives around the world which give us an idea of what to expect in the future.

Machine learning is an application of artificial intelligence (AI) that provides systems with the ability to automatically learn and improve from experience without being explicitly programmed. In other words, it focuses on the development of computer programs that can access a massive quantity of data, find out patterns and use them to learn for themselves. Learning Analytics (LA), or the collection and analysis of traces that learners leave behind, can help to understand and optimise human learning and the environments in which it occurs.

In a school environment, artificial intelligence can be used for four main reasons: security, administration, pedagogical purposes, and grading.

7.1 SECURITY

Artificial Intelligence applied to security is an extension of other forms of technology-based tracking and monitoring. CCTV cameras on campuses for example are getting more and more sophisticated. They do not just film a sequence any more, many of them are based on facial recognition to ensure that no stranger is entering the school compound and to spot any potential criminal. They are already widely spread in the US, UK, Australia and China. Other countries are catching up fast.

An American company called Zero Eyes have developed a smart camera system that can recognise an armed attacker and send an automated alert to local security that includes an image of the suspect with precise details of his location and the weapons he holds.

In many countries, thermal cameras can identify people who have a fever and who could potentially be contagious.

Webcams are also being used for facial recognition to authenticate online learners, confirming that the people engaging in online activities are actually who they claim to be. Along the same lines, AI is used to monitor fake attendance at exams, not only by verifying the identity of the students but also confirming their continued presence throughout the test.

Other administrative and organizational applications include class counting and fingerprint enrollment. Some schools are even considering experimenting with teacher body cameras and RFID (radio-frequency identification) tagging of students.

7.2 ADMINISTRATION

Educators and administrative staff spend a tremendous amount of time getting through school administration. With high application volumes, they often struggle to handle the admissions process. Filtering through this large pool of potential students is often time-intensive, tedious and error-prone. Universities and higher education institutions are using AI-based systems to make this job easier.

AI is also used to answer repetitive inquiries from prospective students or parents. Forward-thinking institutions are using AI powered chatbots or virtual assistants to relieve some of this burden by answering questions about campus, student life and the admissions process.

Some big campuses like Arizona State University are using robots or AI enabled voice assistants to help students learn their way around the first weeks of entering the campus, when they have to familiarise themselves with a new environment and assimilate lots of information.

7.3 EDUCATIONAL PURPOSES

Whereas LMS have focused a lot on equipment or academic content, AI adapted to education claims to help guide children, detect those who are having difficulty in following or put those who have already dropped out back in the loop. As the system gets closer to the student's profile, teachers can propose new working methods more adapted to each child's way of learning. So although adjusting learning based on an individual student's particular needs has been a priority for educators for years, AI will allow a level of differentiation that is impossible for teachers who have to manage thirty students in each class.

For individualized and differentiated learning, AI goes further than facial recognition, it uses facial detection. A growing number of schools are beginning to implement facial detection into commonly used learning platforms such as Moodle, presented in a previous chapter and used by millions of students across the world. In the coming years we are likely to see these practices multiply in the e-learning environment.

The aim is to monitor student's engagement in learning and detect if he or she is having any difficulty in the learning process. Detecting brief facial actions or micro expressions can give indications on the student's engagement or non-engagement in what he or she is studying. The system can highlight in real time periods of boredom, confusion, frustration, surprise or even pleasure. The software can adapt the rhythm and difficulty of activities given to students

The tracking of student learning profile is analyzed and fed back on teacher-dashboards where teachers find relevant information quickly and accurately and derive the right inferences about the needs of their students. But students too can benefit from dashboards. These visual interfaces that capture and visualise traces of learning activities can help them be aware of the way they learn and adjust accordingly by monitoring their own learning methods.

A school in Hangzhou China uses intelligent classroom behaviour management system, which can scan the room every thirty seconds, logging both the behaviour of the students and their facial expressions. The system can identify seven moods, including happy, sad, afraid and angry, by simply analysing a student's face. A camera placed at the front of the classroom, can track six types of behaviour, which include reading, writing, hand raising, standing up, listening to the teacher, and leaning on the desk. One can wonder what is the ultimate goal of this technology. Apparently, it supposed to help track student attendance and assist teachers in adapting their teaching methods. Teachers could benefit from this to optimise their classes and the school to maximize student engagement, but the system could also be used to spy on students and penalize those who are not behaving properly. It could also be a means to intimidate teachers who are less efficient.

AI also helps with educational purposes for home teaching outside the classroom. Many parents are overwhelmed by the content of the home teaching curriculum and can now have the support of AI. Tutoring and studying programmes based on AI respond to a range of learning styles and are becoming more user-friendly. Countries like Australia or the US which have been using homeschooling a lot because of the great distances which are an obstacle to accessing higher education, is benefitting from AI a great deal.

Artificial intelligence can also give universal access insofar as it can bridge the gap between students who speak different languages and those who have visual or hearing impairments. Automatic translator programmes can create subtitles in real time for all students to understand. This also opens up possibilities for students who might not be able to attend school due to illness or who require learning at a different level or on a particular subject that isn't available in their own school

Finally, facial detection can pin point at an early-stage

problems such as dyslexia, autism or ADHD.

7.4 MARKING AND GRADING

The fourth area in which AI has developed is administration, task management and student's productions assessing.

Grading homework and tests is time consuming. AI can step in and make quick work out of these tasks. While computer-assisted marking software has been around for almost as long as computers, it has only been in the last fifteen years or so that computers have begun to be used for marking more abstract students' work, such as argumentative essay writing or written responses to open questions instead of just straightforward multiple-choice or true or false tests.

The classic algorithms of machine learning considered a sequence of keywords. Now deep learning algorithms based on semantic analysis mimic the human ability to understand the meaning of a text and therefore to evaluate students' work. This is what is called text mining or text analytics. The overreaching goal is, essentially, to turn text into data for analysis, via application of Natural Language Processing (NLP) and different kinds of analytical methods.

Numerous schools around the world are experimenting with computer software to grade essays as it seems that the technology can offer the same grade as a human marker up to ninety-two percent of the time. One researcher working on such a project said the machine has evolved continuously and become so complex, we no longer know for sure what it was thinking and how it made a judgment.

China is currently training its neural network grading system in a central server that compiles the work of millions of students. As well as promising a potential way to take out the variations attributed by human subjectivity in marking, this system undoubtedly offers the central government a remarkable ability to track the progress of all students in the country, in real time.

So, all in all we can say that although education might have been a little slow in the adoption of AI and machine learning, it has certainly gone full speed now.

7.5 ETHICAL ISSUES RELATED TO AI

Artificial Intelligence can be frightening in so far as it seems to encompass a whole range of processes that could get out of control if misused. One needs the guarantee that these surveillance and monitoring technologies are not harmful to the students in one way or another and are genuinely beneficial. The pitfalls are numerous. For one, let us keep in mind the dehumanising nature of facially focused schooling if it is taken too far. This can be a very reductive way of considering a person compared to how they would ordinarily be viewed by a human. Making the observations through mathematical algorithms can be abstract and belittling.

I see two problems here, firstly if learners are guided step by step all the time it reduces their freedom of critical thinking and creativity and secondly, jumping to conclusions that a student who looks bored or who is distracted during a course is going to systematically perform badly is also, according to me, a big mistake. For example, some high potential students are sometimes bored because the lesson is not teaching them anything. It is well known for instance that humans can hear and think faster than speech so there is often no need to remain intently focused on what the teacher is saying. Academic attentiveness is not a useful enough predictor of future success to scrutinize it through cameras and to suggest systematic behaviour modification.

Although constant observation would certainly be able to pick out the bullying types and see that they got behavioral training or identify quicker students who would benefit from jumping a class, all this could get out of hand if data was used in any bad way. As a teacher, I must say that in the very first week of getting acquainted with a new class, I can detect these two categories of people very fast without the help of AI.

Also, it should be mandatory that the people who are being put through the AI system are aware of it. The visitors to the Taylor Swift concert at the 2018 Rose Bowl were shocked to find out one year later, that the crowd were surveyed with facial recognition technology.

Keeping in mind that AI has to be handled with care, let us see the more positive sides to it in the classroom with startups that try to merge both the organic and the artificial by applying deep learning systems to education.

7.6 USEFUL AI SOFTWARE

Software such as ClassDojo in the US and Classchart in the UK, already in use in thousands of schools, automates the creation of intelligent class plans that take into account the skills and behaviors of each student.

ClassDojo is an educational technology communication app and website. It connects primary school teachers, students and families through communication features, such as a feed for photos and videos from the school day, and messaging that can be translated into more than thirty-five languages and has been used in numerous countries. It also enables teachers to note feedback on students' skills and creates a portfolio for students, so that families can be aware of school activities outside of meeting with teachers

According to teachers, using ClassDojo's features has "helped demystify" what happens in the classroom for parents. In the United States, one out of every six families with a child in elementary or middle school use ClassDojo's app on a daily basis, and more than nine out of ten of pre-kindergarten through eighth grade schools uses ClassDojo in their classrooms. The features within the app have been compared to a private, ad-free version of Snapchat and Instagram stories, as well as being called the Netflix for education. Other people criticize ClassDojo for teaching "students to understand life as being inseparable from digital technology, and for normalizing surveillance".

Classroom robots that look human are also infiltrating the education industry fast. Pepper and Nao are two good examples of high-tech humanoid robots. Both have been deployed in a variety of industries ranging from retail to healthcare. Pepper has already been adopted by many retailers in Japan, Europe and the United States to welcome customers in an original way. It is capable of informing visitors, orienting them, collecting their level of satisfaction or entertaining them until a salesperson is free. Pepper's versatility has made him able to care for elderly people in nursing homes. What makes Pepper so special is that he is an emotional robot, that is that he will have the most appropriate reaction when faced with an undefined situation. It will have a variety of tones and registers of language that it will select according to the analysis of the context and its interlocutor. The recognition of the interlocutor's emotions is based on the detection of facial expressions, tone and the lexical field that the person uses. In addition to the verbal interaction, the robot will adapt its position and keep a certain distance from the person, so that the person is not uncomfortable, but the relationship can still be built. In the same way, Pepper will adopt a particular body language.

The London Design and Engineering UTC is a new school which focuses on teaching robotics and mechatronics. Pepper and Nao are two of the robots that will be assisting students at the school.

Such robots can be useful in the classroom. As teaching assistants for STEAM (Science, Technology Engineering, Arts and Math), they can serve as customized instructors for individuals or groups, engage with students to enhance social and emotional skills and keep detailed data on their interactions so teachers can track student development.

One of these is called Squirrel and was founded by Yixue Group which specializes in intelligent adaptive education in China. Squirrel AI Learning helps students learn through a real-time adaptive system while cultivating good learning habits with practice. At the very start, students pass a knowledge assessment to establish an intelligence diagnosis in order to detect knowledge gaps or weaknesses. Then a comprehensive knowledge map is set up for each individual so that they can have access to a personalized learning plan and one to one tutoring either with tailored online courses and learning material or with a human teacher. The more students who learn with Squirrel, the more it is possible to personalize the experience and make predictions. Each course is prepared by a team of engineers and teachers who seek to divide the material into an infinite number of conceptual elements. These are then supported by videos, exercises, and other materials. One of the objectives of this technology was to be able to reach schools in remote areas of China where there is a shortage of teachers.

Up to now, Squirrel AI Learning has opened in over one thousand and seven hundred schools and has three thousand teaching staff in more than two hundred cities across more than twenty provinces and autonomous regions in China.

There are many other companies looking at differentiating and individualized learning such as Content Technologies and Carnegie Learning currently developing intelligent instruction design and digital platforms that use AI to provide learning, testing and feedback to students from pre-kindergarten to college level that gives them the challenges they are ready for, identifies gaps in knowledge and redirects to new topics when appropriate. The idea of customizing the curriculum for every student's needs is not viable today, but it will be for AI-powered machines.

Kaspar (which stands for Kinesics and Synchronization in Personal Assistant Robotics) is a project from the University of Hertfordshire. This robot was designed to help teachers and parents support children who have autism or other communication difficulties. Kaspar is a doll-like humanoid the size of a three-year-old child. Its physical appearance is purposely not overly realistic with simple facial features for the children to overcome the complexity of social communication.

Studies have shown that Kaspar can act as a safe and predictable learning tool for children with autism. It enables them to learn social interaction and communication skills and meet specific educational or therapeutic objectives (for example, engaging in direct eye contact or taking turns) in an enjoyable play context. Kaspar can be of help at school, home or in hospitals.

Laurent Jolie, founder of Lalilo invented a system to try to put an end to illiteracy in France. He reminds us that twenty percent of children arriving in sixth grade cannot read. His start up offers a personalized approach to learning to read in a very colourful way. In particular thanks to an algorithm that will determine the mistakes frequently made and make the student rework specific points according to each student. The AI makes it possible to reach many more people thanks to this teaching assistant which helps students who have learning difficulties to learn at their own pace in the classroom.

Vahan is a system to complement instructor-led training for underprivileged communities, helping adults from low-income groups to learn English and improve employability. The approach of its founders is very particular. Rather than focusing on an online solution, they focused on what every Indian has in his or her pocket: a simple mobile phone without an Internet connection. The user will call a number that will contact them immediately, so they do not have to use credit, and they will be able to chat in English with a teacher to improve their language skills. Where the teacher was human at the beginning of the development of the tool, he has now been replaced by this artificial intelligence developed by the start-up. This makes it possible to considerably increase the number of people who can access the service.

Impala is an AI device which is designed to guide young people who want to go to university. This start-up has developed a tool that mixes data science and psychology to help young people find their way. In France, every year, thousands of young people tear their hair out in the meanders of the orientation site Admission Post Bac the National Education platform that allows high school students to choose the institutions they wish to join for their higher education. Impala could help them. Here, artificial intelligence focuses on young people's interests, appetites and expectations and offers them several possible career paths, training courses or institutions that might be suitable for them. The more data the user shares, the more the platform refines its suggestions. Its motto: "You are not just a school file".

Domoscio acts as a personal assistant and enables faster and more sustainable learning. This start-up, created in 2013, bases its approach on three main pillars. The first is "adaptive learning", enabling the assimilation of knowledge through a personalized learning path for each user. The second was christened by the start-up "adaptive anchoring" and corresponds to the memorization and consolidation of knowledge through a repetition of exercises, once again adapted to the rhythm of each learner. Finally, the third point is "the measurement of the impact of learning", thanks to the analysis of the data collected during the entire educational path of the pupil. This last aspect also gives the possibility of setting personalized objectives for each user.

Positioned as a competitor to the American start-up Knewton, Domoscio has been weaving its way into the world of training for the past four years and is now recognised by many institutions like the European Commission and the French Ministry of Education.

In some schools the hyperpersonalization of education

goes even further, like Altschool, for example, founded by Max Ventilla. It is a network of seven schools where every child arrives in the morning with a personalized educational playlist. It works with an AI whose algorithm observes each evening what the student has worked on during the day, in order to propose an adequate program the next day that is non-repetitive and adapted to his needs. The playlists are elaborated in collaboration with the teachers. Every day, the teachers enter their observations on each student into the software in order to "feed" the program.

Some American educators use Nuance, a speech recognition software for their students. The technology can transcribe up to one hundred and sixty words per minute and is useful for those who struggle with writing or have limited mobility. The software also enhances word recognition and spelling ability.

KidSense develops educational AI tools designed specifically for children. The company's speech-to-text tool uses AI to transfer a child's speech into text in order to take notes, practice vocabulary or even take tests. Blippar's products combine computer vision intelligence technology and augmented reality to enhance the way students learn in the classroom. The interactive materials bring subjects like geography, biology and physics to a visual space. For example, instead of reading about volcanic eruption, the system shows students a virtual 3-D model of the eruption process. Thinkster Math is a tutoring program developed for use on laptops, tablets and desktops. The platform combines human interaction with AI to provide students with custom programmes. The AI technology tracks work step-by-step and helps students understand why they are correct or where they went wrong. Querium uses AI to deliver customizable STEM tutoring to high school and college students. By analyzing answers and length of time it took to complete tutoring sessions, Querium's AI gives teachers insights into a student's learning habits and designates areas in which the student could improve.

I could go on and on as new software is produced at an incredible pace. So I will finish this chapter on Artificial Intelligence with a famous anecdote you have probably heard about: Ashok Goel, an American professor who teaches artificial intelligence at the Georgia Institute of Technology in the US finally told his students that Jill Watson, his assistant professor, was actually an AI. The four hundred students in her online course had sent her about ten thousand messages. "Jill Watson" had handled forty percent of all the questions without any of the students realising that she was not human!

Behind all this use of technology there is always the same objective, that of handing the learning to the students. Finland is leading the way with one of the most innovative and radical education reform programmes ever implemented by a state. The reform aims to put an end to subject teaching and the conventional teacher-pupil board by proposing a more collaborative approach called Phenomena Based Learning. This involves bringing students together in several small groups and giving them problems to solve or complex phenomena to grasp, such as global warming for example, in order to encourage teamwork and communication.

Similarly, Stanford University says it wants to end its teaching majors by 2025 and reinvent its teaching around "Missions". Students, guided by a professor turned mentor, will form ad hoc groups around complex problems and use different sources of knowledge, technologies, and disciplines to advance their mission. This is similar to the concept of Purpose Learning. Becoming "neuroeducators", tomorrow's teachers will have the mission of boosting intellectual and creative capacities by making human and artificial intelligences complementary.

CONCLUSION

Because of Covid-19 which hit us all in March 2020, traditional teachers all around the world, and I was one of them, had to start remote teaching overnight. All educational staff were suddenly put through an experience we imagined may come one day or another but for which many of us were totally unprepared.

But if our adaptability was put to the test, developing strategies for moving our classes online, there is another consequence that was much more significant in my opinion and that is the reaction of the students themselves when deprived of their teacher's physical presence.

For younger children in primary school, it was like a sudden estrangement. They were completely destabilized and felt abandoned proving that, even in today's digital world, hands-on learning with a qualified teacher is vital for development, particularly early on.

For older ones, after having experienced an initial exhilarating feeling of freedom, little by little they started telling their teachers that they missed something they could not really define despite the continual online contact. Teenagers I was working with were not all ready or able to monitor this suddenly acquired solitude. Some of them just dropped out of the system for three main reasons: lack of technology in the home, lack of parental support or difficulty in structuring their own learning-program. Many of them said that they missed the social connection with their peers but the underlying statement was clearly that they also missed the guidance represented by physical teachers.

Very quickly, teachers' social role was recognised for what it is: a profession that has an essential role in society just like that of medical careers, cleaners, policemen and other jobs that are too often overlooked because they are taken for granted. Moreover, the Covid-19 experience has shown us all that not only we have to be ready for a future pandemic but we have to explore teleworking very seriously and get remote teaching right.

Knowing that teachers are available online is not the same as being able to go and see them and actually talk to them. The reassurance teachers can provide to students cannot be replaced. I quickly realised that the messages I was sending them through Google Classroom, Meet or WhatsApp were not replacing my presence in the classroom. The physical and human presence remains irreplaceable.

To come back to the moto mentioned at the beginning of the book, if the best teacher is the one who inspires, one can only do this with some minimal human contact, relationship and exchange. If the only connection between a student and a teacher is a software, this inspiration will be limited. Even if virtual documents can have some kind of personal signature or mark, they will never totally replace the personality and charisma of a human being. The physical presence of teachers will reassure those who believe too much time with digital devices disconnects students from face-to-face social activities, family communications, and nature.

It is highly likely that the best future educators will be coaches, empathetic and therefore humane, treating their students as equals. Even technologies based on augmented reality will not replace the human in education, but will bring them closer. In this new era of education online, prerogatives such as time management, cognitive ergonomics, information literacy and citizenship but also concentration, transformational learning and mindfulness are only some among many elements that will have to be taken into account on a daily basis.

So do teachers still have a role in a world where remote learning is omnipresent and where intelligence is no longer limited?

As I have tried to show in my analysis the answer is definitely yes, both on the human and on a technical level. It is not a question of replacing teachers with the all-technological, but rather of evolving their mission. In the future their main role will not just be the simple transmission of knowledge with all the implications this has, but rather the creation in their students of favourable dispositions of curiosity, creativity and collaboration to navigate comfortably in a complex and changing world. As competing with machines in the technical and scientific fields is totally pointless it will be necessary to rehabilitate creativity, humanities, social skills, and general culture at the heart of the education system. Finding ways to effectively utilize digital devices in the classroom provides teachers with an opportunity to advance their skillset and grow with their students. Many teachers are already taking their digital literacy to the next level by earning a master's degree in education technology. According to UNESCO, the world is already facing a shortage of teachers and by 2030, countries will need to recruit a total of sixty-nine million additional teachers worldwide so teachers will always be needed and even more so, digitally competent ones.

Human and silicon brains have to cohabit because human and artificial intelligence are going to be complementary. What is new however is that for the first time our students are more at ease with the tools we are trying to adapt to therefore the interaction between teachers and students is going to blossom into something new, pushed forward by technology. We can all teach one another and move forward together. And as learning will be more personalized, the personal skills, aptitudes and abilities of both students and teachers will be more than ever crucial.

The bottom line is that the digitalization of education is just an enabler. Very good digital products are paradoxically the ones that most resemble humans. Therefore, the relationship between the teacher and the student will always be the foundation of successful teaching.

BIBLIOGRAPHY

Agarwal, A. The Developing World of MOOCs: MIT (Linc 2013 conference video: 1hr 34 mins in.) Boston, 2013.

Anderson, C. The End of Theory: The Data Deluge Makes the Scientific Method Obsolete. Wired Magazine, 16.07.2008

Baron, Dennis A Better Pencil. Readers, Writers and the Digital Revolution. Oxford University Press. USA, 2012.

Baron, George-Louis, Réflexions sur les TIC en éducation. Formation et profession, Bulletin du CRIFPE, vol. 12, no 3, 2006, p. 12-16.

Baron, Naomi S. Always On: Language in an Online and Mobile World. Oxford University Press. New York, 2008.

Baron, Naomi S. Words Onscreen. The Fate of Reading in a Digital World. Oxford University Press. New York, 2015

Bates, A. Teaching, Open Learning and Distance Education London/New York: Routledge, 1995

Bates, Tony. Pedagogical roles for video in online learning. Online Learning and Distance Education Resources, March 10. 2012.

Bates Tony. What is right and what is wrong with Coursera-style MOOCs Online Learning and Distance Education Resources, August 5, 2012

Bates Tony, Swennen Anja, Jones Ken. The Professional Development of Teacher Educators. Routledge, 2012.

Bertrand, Annie et Garnier, Pierre-Henri, Psychologie cognitive, Levallois Perret, Jeunes Éditions-Studyrama, 2005.

Besançon, Véronique et Dubeau, Annie, Environnement WebCT: des outils pour enseigner et apprendre, Dossiers pratiques Profetic, 2005.

Sir Blaydon Barber, Michael. The Learning Game: Arguments for an

Education Revolution (Indigo, 1997). References- David Hargreaves, The Mosaic of Learning, Demos, 1994- Michael Fullan, Change Forces: The Sequel, Falmer Press, 1999.

Blitman, Sophie. Ce que l'intelligence artificielle peut apporter à l'éducation. Publié sur le Monde 23 mars, 2017.

Boyd, Robert D., and Myers, J. Gordon. Transformative Education. International Journal of Lifelong Education 7, no. 4 (October— December 1988): 261–284.

Broda Tamburi, Susan Jane. Power, Beauty and Legitimacy of Adolescence. Clinkstreet. London/ New York, 2019.

Brookfield, S.D. (2000). Transformative learning as ideology critique. In J. Mezirow & Associates (Eds.), Learning as transformation. Critical perspectives on a theory in progress (pp. 125–150). San Francisco, CA: Jossey-Bass.

Carey, K. The End of College New York: Riverhead Books. New York, 2015.

Charron, Sylvain. Divided Representation of Concurrent Goals in the Human Frontal Lobes. Science, Vol. 328. no. 5976, pp. 360–363

Cheung, King Sing. A comparison of WebCT, Blackboard and Moodle for the Teaching and Learning of Continuing Education course, in P. Tsang, R. Kwan et R. Fox (dir.), Enhancing Learning through Technology, World Scientific Publishing, 2007, p. 219–228.

Christensen, C. (2010) Disrupting Class, Expanded Edition: How Disruptive Innovation Will Change the Way the World Learns New York: McGraw-Hill

Dabbagh, N. (2007). The Online Learner: characteristics and pedagogical implications. Contemporary Issues in Technology and Teacher Education, Vol. 7, No. 3, pp 217–226.

Dewey, John and Evelyne, Schools of tomorrow. Franklin Classic 2018.

Dirkx, J.M.; Mezirow, J.; Cranton, P. Musings and reflections on the meaning, context, and process of transformative learning: A dialogue between John M. Dirkx and Jack Mezirow Journal of Transformative Education. 2006

Hayles, N. Katherine (2007). Hyper and Deep Attention: The Generational Divide in Cognitive Modes. Profession, 2007, pp. 187–199 (13). Published by: Modern Language Association

Mezirow, J. "Perspective Transformation". Adult Education Quarterly. 28 (2). 1978

Palmer, P. The Courage to Teach: Exploring the Inner Landscape of a Teacher's Life. Wiley: San Francisco, 2007.

Robinson, Sir Ken and Aronica Lou. The Element: How Finding your Passion changes Everything. Penguin Edition. London, 2010.

Robinson, Sir Ken. Finding your Element: how to discover your passions and talents and transform your life. Penguin. London, 2014.

Robinson, Sir Ken. Out of our Minds: The power of being Creative. Published by John Wiley & Sons Ltd. UK, 2017.

Sylvain Charron and Etienne Koechlin (2010). Divided Representation of Concurrent Goals in the Human Frontal Lobes. Science, Vol. 328. no. 5976, pp. 360–363.

Daniela, Linda. Pedagogies of Digital Learning in Higher Education (perspectives on Education in the Digital Age). English Education. Routledge 2020

D'Amour Véronique: Le multitâche et l'apprentissage. Published 15 fFebruary 2010. Adapeted from The Divided Attention, published in The chronicle of Higher Education 31 January 2010.

D'Amour Véronique: L'illusion de la performance au détriment de l'efficacité. "Ethique et TICS en classe. 14 mars 2010.

-Desmet Piet, L'enseignement/apprentissage des langues à l'ère du numérique: tendances récentes et défis, Revue française de linguistique appliquée, vol. XI, no 1, 2006, p. 119-138.

Erikson, Erik H. Childhood and Society.2d ed., rev. WW. Norton, New York,1963 (first edition 1950).

Erikson, Erik H. Identity: Youth and Crisis. The University of Machigan. W.W Norton & Company, New York,1968.

Erikson, Erik H. Identity and the Life Circle. WW.Norton & Company, International Universtities Press, Inc. New York, 1994.

Erikson, Erik H. Life Circle Completed. W.W. Norton G Company, New York, 1998.

Hayles, N. Katherine, Hyper and Deep Attention: The Generational Divide in Cognitive Modes. Published by Modern Language Association. 2007

Heutte Jean, Le travail de recherche documentaire et de production collective en ligne: propositions pour l'intégration pragmatique, progressive et incrémentale des technologies numériques dans les pratiques enseignantes, Revue internationale des technologies en pédagogie universitaire, vol. 7, no 2, 2010, p.48–59.

Hoc Jean-Michel, L'ergonomie cognitive un compromis nécessaire entre des approches centrées sur la machine et des approches centrées sur l'homme, dans Y. Quéinnec (dir.), Actes du colloque

« Recherche et ergonomie » (Toulouse), 1998

Klingberg, Torkel. Memory and Brain Development in Children. Oxford University Press. 2013

Klingberg, Torkel. The overflowing Brain: information Overload and the limits of working Memory. Oxford University Press. 2009.

Livingstone Sonia and Alicia Blum Ross. Parenting for a Digital Future. Oxford University Press 2020.

Marcia, James E. Development and Validation of Ego-Identity Status, in: Journal of Personality and Social Psychology Vol.3, no.5, 1996.

Marcia, James E. Ego-Identity Status in Argyle, Michael. Social Encounters. Penguin. London, 1977. p.340–354.

Mayeroff, Milton. On Caring. Harper & Row. New York, 1971.

Morrison Mary Kay Using Humour to maximize learning. Kindle Edition. 2008.

Noddings, Nel. Caring: A Feminine Approach to Ethics and Moral

Education. Berkeley University of California Press. Berkeley, 1984.

Ophir, E., Nass, C & Wagner, A.D. Cognitive control in media multitaskers. 2009.

Scardamalia, M. and Bereiter, C. Knowledge Building: Theory, pedagogy and technology, in Sawyer, K. (ed.) Cambridge Handbook of the Learning Sciences New York: Cambridge University Press. 2009.

Tijus, Charles & Blancher Alain. Introduction à la psychologie cognitive. Edition Nathan. Paris, 2001.

Sylvie Vandaele, Nouvelles technologies et enseignement: progrès ou illusion? http://journals.openedition.org/ilcea/1033; DOI: 10.4000/ilcea.1033

Trenaman, J. Communication and Comprehension London: Longmans. London, 1967

Weinstein Yana, Sumerack Megan, Caviglioli Oliver Understanding how we learn. Routledge. New York, 2019.

Woodley, A. and Simpson, O. (2014) 'Student drop-out: the elephant in the room' in Zawacki-Richter, O. and Anderson, T. (eds.) (2014) Online Distance Education: Towards a Research Agenda.Athabasca AB: AU Press, pp. 508

Divided Representation of Concurrent Goals in the Human Frontal Lobes. Science, Vol. 328. no. 5976, pp. 360–363.

Lightning Source UK Ltd.
Milton Keynes UK
UKHW010335250122
397665UK00001B/9